Information Literacy and Theological Librarianship: Theory & Praxis

EDITED BY BOBBY SMILEY

ATLA OPEN PRESS

Chicago - 2019

atla Open Press

Published by Atla Open Press, An Imprint of the American Theological
Library Association (Atla), 300 South Wacker Drive, Suite 2100,
Chicago, IL 60606-6701 USA

Published in the United States of America in 2019.

ISBN-13 978-1-949800-01-2 (PDF)

ISBN-13 978-1-949800-02-9 (EPUB)

ISBN-13 978-1-949800-03-6 (Cloth)

Cover Design: Lisa Buckley

Contents

Introduction

BOBBY SMILEY, VANDERBILT UNIVERSITY

> *The greatest defect in theological education today is that it is too much an affair of piecemeal transmission of knowledge and skills, and that, in consequence, it offers too little challenge to the student to develop [their] own resources and to become an independent, lifelong inquirer, growing constantly while [the student] is engaged in the work of the ministry.*[1]
>
> – H. Richard Niebuhr, *The Advancement of Theological Education* (1957)

*I*N 1983, SOME THIRTY YEARS BEFORE THE ASSOCIATION OF COLLEGE AND Research Libraries (ACRL) released the first draft of the *Framework for Information Literacy in Higher Education* (the *Framework*), the idea of frameworks for teaching and learning in theological libraries was already being proposed. In a paper entitled "The Structures of Religious Literature: Conceptual Frameworks for Improving Bibliographic Instruction" at Atla's 37th Annual conference, Andrew D. Scrimgeour, then the director of the Ira J. Taylor Library at Illif School of Theology, accented "the importance of cognitive structures, or frameworks, in the learning process."[2] This invocation of "frameworks" didn't seem merely adventitious or just rhetorically convenient. Indeed, Scrimgeour acknowledges in his address the influence of Raymond McInnis, a longtime reference and instruction librarian from Western Washington University and theorist of library pedagogy, whose approach was informed by instructional psychology, and who emphasized building library instruction around conceptual structures and disciplinary research strategies. [3]

As befits a theological librarian, Scrimgeour cites the above epigraph from H. Richard Niebuhr as an "indictment of the seminary enterprise [that] also indexes my efforts in bibliographic instruction."[4] Chronicling his pedagogical progression from a greenhorn "magician" librarian (the whiz with sources) to more of a teacherly "guide" (focusing on search strategies), he offers commentary that might strike a reader today as surprisingly contemporary, if not proleptic of current discussion about frameworks and threshold concepts. Using concepts, he explains, aids intelligibility, provides structure, and situates whatever concept is being addressed in conversation with already familiar concepts, thereby activating student learning. And he also echoes McInnis's stress on student learning as an iterative and associative process, in implied contrast to student learning as rote mastery. As Niebuhr himself suggests in *The Advancement of Theological Education*'s assessment of instruction in theological libraries, "[m]ost schools provide an orientation session in the library at the beginning of the course, and this has value, but hardly touches the need to discover the working relationship between the classroom and library."[5] Scrimgeour's paper deftly encapsulates the intellectual energy and attention given to creative instruction that theological librarians have long exhibited in their efforts to work with students to make that "working relationship between the classroom and library" more durable.

* * *

I start the introduction to *Information Literacy and Theological Librarianship: Theory and Praxis* with this particular historical excursus to highlight how theological and religious studies librarians have long been engaged in discussions and innovations in library instruction and how, along with their educational context, that imperative for innovation was shaped by figures and scholars in religion, as well as peers in the profession. By looking to instructional psychology, the work of librarians like McInnis offered his colleagues in theological librarianship a theoretical matrix within which to challenge and reimagine how their instruction could be more effective and enduring. What Scrimgeour's paper adumbrates is, in many ways, a prescient theoretical engagement of what was then labeled "bibliographic instruction" and is now more often branded as "information literacy"[6] (see Image 1).

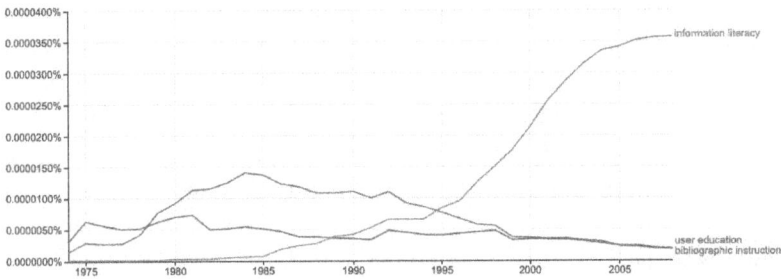

IMAGE 1 Google n-gram graph of library instruction terms, 1974–2008.

Although the term "information literacy" is of relatively recent vintage, the idea of library "user education" has formative nineteenth-century antecedents. Writing in 1880, Boston Public's and Harvard Library's Justin Winsor and the University of Rochester's Otis Hall Robinson argued that library instruction for user education must focus "special attention on the *how* and *where* of [knowledge] acquisition" [emphasis in the original].[7] Indeed, Robinson underscored the import of "hands-on" experience for students, and articulated at the American Library Association's annual conference in 1881 three objectives all library instruction should strive to achieve: the need to "develop the art of discrimination" by judging the value of books to develop critical judgment, for students to become independent learners who teach themselves, and thereby become lifelong learners.[8] But for Robinson, and other contemporaries active in library pedagogy, like Raymond C. Davis of the University of Michigan, a premium was placed on the *bibliographic* side of instruction: that is, imparting technical mastery of the card catalog and classification schema and knowledge of reference sources to students in the librarian's capacity as a "professor of books."[9] Even for twentieth-century advocates and innovators, such as Evan Ira Farber, who pushed for greater curricular integration (even called for by Robinson in 1880), library instruction still rested more on the materials to be sourced and less on cultivating critical judgement and "the art of discrimination."[10]

Contemporary usage of "information literacy" is often traced to Paul G. Zurkowski's 1974 white paper for the National Commission on Libraries and Information Science, *The Information Service Environment Relationships and Priorities.*[11] "[I]nformation literates," Zurkowski explained, possessed "techniques and skills" in the "application of information resources" and "information solutions" used for problem solving.[12] In contradistinction to bibliographic instruction, the concept of information literacy reoriented learning from the primacy of books to how the learner could discern and navigate myriad sources and types of information. Echoing Zurkowski, the Association of College and Research Libraries proclaimed in 1989 that information literacy was an information age "survival skill."[13] And by 2000, ACRL released *Information Literacy Competency Standards for Higher Education*, a comprehensive document detailing techiques and skills for infomation literacy, which displaced their earlier "Model Statement of Objectives for Academic Bibliographic Instruction" (1979, 1987).[14]

Since its initial circulation in draft form in February 2014, *The Framework for Information Literacy in Higher Education* (officially adopted by ACRL in 2016) has transformed the conversation around information literacy instruction from mastery of standards and discrete performance indicators to more flexible approaches grounded in threshold concepts. Whereas the *Information Literacy Competency Standards* provided a highly structured task-list of learning objectives, the *Framework* concentrated on more abstract approaches for stimulating critical judgement that valorizes the role of the learner over the skill. Centered around six "frames" (Authority Is Constructed and Contextual, Information Creation as a Process, Information Has Value, Research as Inquiry, Scholarship as Conversation, and Searching as Strategic Exploration), the document makes an argument for how foundational concepts in information literacy can be (as Jan Meyer and Ray Land describe threshold concepts) transformative, irreversible, integrative, bounded and troublesome.[15]

As a relatively freshly minted librarian at the time the draft *Framework* was first released, I found the conceptual approach animating the document theoretically consonant with the pedagogical techniques I learned as a secondary school teacher. In particular, it was easier and more intelligible for me to crosswalk threshold concepts in own home discipline of American religious history, as well as religious studies and history, to information literacy frames, like "Scholarship as Conversation" (around which one of this volume's contributors, Kaeley McMahan, bases her chapter). Identifying those parallels and building library instruction around twinned disciplinary and information literacy threshold concepts, I've been able to be imaginative with more applied and authentic assignments that balance the instrumental and intrinsic value of even meat-and-potatoes library learning (e.g. databases and the catalog); that is to say, I'm able to teach an information literacy frame through a threshold concept in a disciplinary context by designing an activity that requires library resources to do exactly what professionals do for their research and writing.[16] While not unproblematic, the *Framework*'s embrace of threshold concepts nevertheless helped punch out a pedagogical space for me to be inventive while also giving me wider berth to leverage my domain expertise.[17] Confronted with a laundry list of standards and performance indicators, I doubt I would be as creative or immediately apt to envision how disciplinary concepts and information literacy could be placed in dialogue meaningful to both.

That meaningful dialogue is the genesis of this book, and the contributions are illustrations of how that dialogue can be contemplated and achieved. Marshalling personal experiences, best practices, and theoretical explorations unique to religious studies and theological librarianship, this volume places both areas in conversation with the *Framework*. The subtitle of this volume, *Theory and Praxis*, embodies the complementary ways the contributors successfully reckoned with the influence of the *Framework* on information literacy in the multiple educational settings where theological and religious studies librarians work. And so *Information Literacy and Theological Librarianship* includes librarians working in seminaries, small liberal arts colleges, regional religious universities, as well as divinity schools that are part of R1 schools. While not unique, that kind of institutional plurality is profoundly important to theological librarianship, only matched by the equal import of the library's role in the student's intellectual and professional trajectory, as well as, often, their devotional and vocational path.

In his second thesis from *Theses on Feuerbach*, Karl Marx argues that "thinking that is isolated from practice is ... purely *scholastic*,"[18] and it is this productive tension that contributors from the "Theory" section hold in equipoise: whether revealing and interrogating the suppositions of instruction (Osinski), understanding our information ecosystem (Kuehn), reimagining our teaching with international students in mind (Veldheer), or descrying connections between theological disciplines and information literacy (Badke). And if theory is speaking to practice in *Information Literacy and Theological Librarianship*'s first half, then in "Praxis," practice, in the form of case studies, is enlisted to theorize concretely: by curriculum mapping for existing courses (Miller), reimagining and rearticulating information literacy principles and policies (Board), leading credit-bearing courses (McMahan, LeBlanc and Tsonos), or teaching with special collections material (Anderson and Stetler).

While the body of scholarly and practical literature around the *Framework* is already large (and growing), there's a comparatively exiguous amount of work examining both contemporary information literacy practices and theory as well as theological and religious studies librarianship (and some of that work done by contributors to this volume). *Information Literacy and Theological Librarianship* provides the first sustained *Framework*-era intervention, and I hope it will be a bellwether for future mediations on the instructional challenges and opportunities unique to our specialization, as well as those common to all library colleagues in higher education.

Bibliography

Behrens, Shirley J. "A Conceptual Analysis and Historical Overview of Information Literacy" *College & Research Libraries,* 55 No. 4 (1 July 1994): 309–320.

Framework for Information Literacy for Higher Education. Chicago: Association of College and Research Libraries, 2015.

Hernon, Peter. "Instruction in the Use of Academic Libraries: A Preliminary Study of the Early Years as Based on Selective Extant Materials." *The Journal of Library History,* 17, No. 1 (Winter, 1982): 16–38.

Marx, Karl. "Theses on Feuerbach." In *Early Writings,* translated by Rodney Livingstone and Gregor Benton. London: Penguin Press, 1992.

McInnis, Raymond J. *New Perspectives for Reference Services in Academic Libraries.* Westport, CT: Greenwood Press, 1978.

McMahon, Melody Layton and David R. Stewart. *A Broadening Conversation: Classic Readings in Theological Librarianship.* Lanham, MD: Scarecrow Press, 2006.

Meyer, Jan H. F. and Ray Land. "Threshold Concepts and Troublesome Knowledge (2): Epistemological Considerations and a Conceptual Framework for Teaching and Learning." *Higher Education,* 49 (2005): 373–88.

Niebuhr, H. Richard, Daniel Day Williams, and James M. Gustafson. *The Advancement of Theological Education.* New York: Harper & Brothers, 1957.

Presidential Committee on Information Literacy: Final Report. Chicago: Association of College and Research Libraries, 1989.

Robinson, Otis H. and Justin Winsor. "College Libraries as Aids to Instruction." In *Circulars of Information of the Bureau of Education, no. 1–1880.* Washington, D.C., United States Government Printing Office, 1880.

Saracevic, Tefko. "Information Literacy in the United States: Contemporary Transformations and Controversies." In *Information Literacy: Lifelong Learning and Digital Citizenship in the 21st Century: Second European Conference, ECIL 2014, Dubrovnik, Croatia, October 20–23, 2014,* edited by Serap Kurbanoğlu, S. Špiranec, E. Grassian, D. Mizrachi, and R. Catts, 19–30. Cham: Springer International Publishing, 2014.

Scrimgeour, Andrew D. "The Structures of Religious Literature: Conceptual Frameworks for Improving Bibliographic Instruction." In *A Broadening Conversation: Classic Readings in Theological Librarianship,* edited by Melody Layton McMahon and David R. Stewart, 162–8. Lanham, MD: Scarecrow Press, 2006.

Smiley, Bobby. "Crosswalking the Disciplines: Reimagining Information Literacy Instruction for a History Methods Course." In *The Grounded Instruction*

Librarian: Participating in The Scholarship of Teaching and Learning, edited by Melissa Mallon, Lauren Hays, Cara Bradley, Rhonda Huisman, and Jackie Belanger, 43–52. Chicago: Association of College and Research Libraries, 2019.

Tibbo, Helen. "User Instruction Issues for Database Searching in the Humanities." In *Encyclopedia of Library and Information Science*, vol. 65, supp. 28, edited by Allen Kent, 330–354. New York: CRC Press, 1999.

Tucker, J. M. "The Origins of Bibliographic Instruction in Academic Libraries, 1876–1914." In *New Horizons for Academic Libraries*, edited by R. D. Stueart and R. D. Johnson, 268–276. New York: K.G. Saur Verlang, 1979.

Wilkinson, Lane. "The Problem with Threshold Concepts." *Sense and Reference* (blog), June 19, 2014. *https://senseandreference.wordpress.com/2014/06/19/the-problem-with-threshold-concepts/*

Zurkowski, Paul G. *The Information Environment: Relationships and Priorities*. Washington, DC: National Commission on Libraries and Information Science, 1974.

Notes

1. H. Richard Niebuhr, Daniel Day Williams, and James M. Gustafson, *The Advancement of Theological Education* (New York: Harper & Brothers, 1957), 209, quoted in Andrew D. Scrimgeour, "The Structures of Religious Literature: Conceptual Frameworks for Improving Bibliographic Instruction," in *A Broadening Conversation: Classic Readings in Theological Librarianship*, eds. Melody Layton McMahon and David R. Stewart (Lanham, MD: Scarecrow Press, 2006), 163.

2. Scrimgeour, 164.

3. See Raymond J. McInnis, *New Perspectives for Reference Services in Academic Libraries* (Westport, CT: Greenwood Press, 1978).

4. Scrimgeour, 164.

5. Niebuhr, Williams, and Gustafson, 129. But let's not credit Niebuhr et al. with too much insight or even good sense about instruction. In a section risibly titled "Teaching Methods," just a few paragraphs down on the same page as the epigraph, the authors aver in language redolent with gendered contempt that "a student-centered pedagogue is not a teacher, but a nurse."

6. The conflation of terms, I would argue, is a specious equivalence.

7. Otis H. Robinson and Justin Winsor, "College Libraries as Aids to Instruction," in *Circulars of Information of the Bureau of Education, no. 1–1880* (Washington, D.C., United States Government Printing Office, 1880), 21.

8. J. M. Tucker, "The Origins of Bibliographic Instruction in Academic Libraries, 1876–1914," in *New Horizons for Academic Libraries*, eds. R. D. Stueart and R. D. Johnson (New York: K.G. Saur Verlang, 1979), 271.

9. Peter Hernon, "Instruction in the Use of Academic Libraries: A Preliminary Study of the Early Years as Based on Selective Extant Materials," *The Journal of Library History* 17, no. 1 (Winter, 1982): 20.

10. Helen Tibbo, "User Instruction Issues for Database Searching in the Humanities," in *Encyclopedia of Library and Information Science*, vol. 65, supp. 28, ed. Allen Kent (New York: CRC Press, 1999), 332.

11. Shirley J. Behrens, "A Conceptual Analysis and Historical Overview of Information Literacy," *College & Research Libraries* 55, no. 4 (1 July 1994): 310.

12. Paul G. Zurkowski, *The Information Environment: Relationships and Priorities* (Washington, DC: National Commission on Libraries and Information Science, 1974), 6.

13. *Presidential Committee on Information Literacy: Final Report* (Chicago: Association of College and Research Libraries, 1989), as quoted in Tefko Saracevic, "Information Literacy in the United States: Contemporary Transformations and Controversies," in *Information Literacy: Lifelong Learning and Digital Citizenship in the 21st Century: Second European Conference, ECIL 2014, Dubrovnik, Croatia, October 20–23, 2014*, eds. Serap Kurbanoğlu et al. (Cham: Springer International Publishing, 2014), 20.

14. Saracevic, 20.

15. Jan H. F. Meyer and Ray Land, "Threshold Concepts and Troublesome Knowledge (2): Epistemological Considerations and a Conceptual Framework for Teaching and Learning," *Higher Education* 49 (2005): 373–88.

16. See Bobby Smiley, "Crosswalking the Disciplines: Reimagining Information Literacy Instruction for a History Methods Course," in *The Grounded Instruction Librarian: Participating in The Scholarship of Teaching and Learning*, eds. Melissa Mallon, Lauren Hays, Cara Bradley, Rhonda Huisman, and Jackie Belanger (Chicago: Association of College and Research Libraries, 2019), 43–52.

17. For a philosophical critque of the *Framework*'s use of threshold concepts, see Lane Wilkinson, "The Problem with Threshold Concepts," *Sense and Reference* (blog), June 19, 2014, https://senseandreference.wordpress.com/2014/06/19/the-problem-with-threshold-concepts/.

18. Karl Marx, "Theses on Feuerbach," in *Early Writings*, trans. Rodney Livingstone and Gregor Benton (London: Penguin Press, 1992), 422.

Theory

CHAPTER 1

Exposing the Null Curriculum in Graduate Religious Education

KEEGAN OSINSKI, VANDERBILT UNIVERSITY

G RADUATE EDUCATION AND ACADEMIC SCHOLARSHIP ARE RIDDLED WITH expectations–both those delineated in syllabi and tenure requirements and those underlying, tacit expectations that create an implicit culture that is challenging to name and untangle. For students especially, who are learning to navigate the academic environment at the beginning of their careers, trying to meet expectations, achieve goals, and earn grades, parsing the unspoken expectations of academia can be frustrating and seemingly impossible and can create a major barrier to success. Librarians, who are within the academic system and yet inhabit a third space separate from the faculty/student dichotomy, are uniquely situated to understand the mechanics of the academy and communicate them in a way that is accessible and effective.

This essay will discuss some of the implicit assumptions placed on students, how they come to be and what effect they have, and the challenges presented to both students and faculty because of the unspokenness of requirements and expectations. It will also propose possible solutions to these challenges, suggesting ways librarians, in their particular position, can address these assumptions to make them explicit and support students in their academic flourishing.

The data for this essay is primarily anecdotal, gleaned from a variety of both formal and informal conversations with graduate students of religion, professors of various ranks and seniority, and librarians, from a variety of institutions–community college, state schools, and private universities from small to large, liberal arts to R-1. In analyzing notes from these conversations, several themes became apparent. Issues arose around the following: foundations–where students came from and the background knowledge they arrived at school with, as well as the goals they had for their education; writing–assumptions of skills and abilities and the standards of the discipline; reading–how students approach and analyze texts; and the general culture of shame engendered by the academic environment. Because these issues are so often at play under the surface of education and academic work, it can be hard to talk about them explicitly, but I'm confident that they will resonate as recognizable concerns that are virtually universal in higher education. To make plain these unspoken issues is the first step in bringing them to light so that they might be addressed in our institutions and result in a more fulfilling and successful academic experience for both students and faculty.

Foundations

Graduate theological education benefits from the broad diversity of backgrounds from which our students come to us. I've known students to enter divinity school with degrees in everything from chemistry, engineering, and physics, to English, international business, and psychology. This range of experiences is often a boon for the community, resulting in rich and lively conversations, but the variety of perspectives also means a variety of skill levels, abilities, and approaches to academic work that may lend themselves more or less readily to religion specifically. Some students come to graduate school with a solid foundation of subject knowledge and context, while others are being introduced to the vocabulary and key figures for the first time. Some students are comfortable analyzing texts and writing research papers, while others are unfamiliar with the mechanics of humanities work. For many students pursuing ministry as a second career or a later-in-life calling, returning to school means learning anew how to manage coursework and educational technology. International students encounter any and all of these challenges, in addition to working in a foreign culture and language.

Not all students come to graduate school properly prepared for the road ahead of them. The amount of reading and writing can be a shock and can take significant adjustment. If students come from a different discipline or perhaps did not initially plan to pursue graduate work, they may not feel confident or ready for its academic challenges. The tricks of the trade, as it were, that are picked up over years of practice seem to be second nature and are taken for granted by faculty and more experienced and prepared students. If these skills are not taught explicitly, we do a disservice to a significant portion of our student population and risk leaving them behind. This issue is exacerbated by factors like race and class–students from wealthy backgrounds have the luxury of increased preparation, tutoring, and other resources that put them ahead. First generation students may not have the benefit of parents or other mentors teaching them what to expect and how to achieve their academic goals. In order to level the playing field and bring all students up to speed, it's essential that educators make plain the skills and expectations that are required for success.

Beyond the differences in background, students also have differences in goals. Their assumptions of the purpose and trajectory of their programs can differ widely, both from each other and also from those of the faculty and the administration. Because degrees in theology and religious studies are lauded as versatile, with career options in ministry, nonprofit, academic work, and more, students come to their work with different reasons for why they are there, and this can be at odds with other students and faculty. Academically-minded students may struggle with "practical" courses or assignments, while ministry-focused students may be frustrated by more heavily theoretical work.

Much of the conflict in backgrounds and goals is unspoken–either regarded as unimportant and therefore unaddressed, or simply ignored, undetected, or uninterrogated. The challenge that emerges again and again for educators in this context is how to get so many different people on the same academic page. Again, I believe the solution lies in making the implicit explicit. Laying bare the expectations. Setting a common baseline. There should be a clear explanation of what students can expect out of their program–what they will learn and what they won't, what will be attended to in the classroom and what should be addressed elsewhere.

A common concern to this effect, particularly in divinity schools that are training ministers, is the spiritual and emotional wellbeing of students. There are often conflicting expectations regarding "pastoral care" in the classroom, as well as additional support for students struggling with questions of deep significance to their own religious life. Programs and schools that are not clear about where, when, and how these kinds of conversations are handled will face dissatisfaction, discomfort, and disappointment on the part of both students and faculty. Further, other support staff (including librarians) often will be expected to perform the additional emotional labor of guiding and counseling students, and whether that labor is recognized and officially expected makes a difference in the way their professional vocations are carried out and again affects the experience and outcomes of students.

Even within the single field of religious studies there are multiple disciplines, each with their own ethos and conventions. For example, biblical studies, theology, and religious anthropology are vastly different areas. Students need to be taught how to interact with the texts and do the kind of work expected in each area. Skills don't always translate directly between classes or assignments, and explicit instruction is how students will become acquainted with the disciplines. It is unrealistic and unfair to expect students to pick up the subtleties and specialized ways of thinking, particularly at the master's level, and especially if it is their first introduction to the discipline. For many students, graduate work begins as an exploration of possibilities. Students need definitions of and training in the different genres of academic writing and different kinds of classes, and this instruction needs to be clear and explicit. Educators should take the opportunity to properly introduce the discipline and its attendant expectations and protocols. Not only will students then have a more complete understanding and appreciation of the subject and its scholarly context, but they will also be better equipped for success in the class itself.

While much of this work must be done at an administrative, department level –visioning clear program goals, setting specific student learning outcomes–some of the practical execution of establishing a cohesive academic program can benefit greatly from librarian involvement. Librarians can help translate the expectations and goals into actionable programming for student learning.

One possibility for setting a foundational standard would be a pre-matriculation "boot camp," where students are told explicitly what to expect as well as what is expected of them. This can entail more discursive topics, such as the practical/academic "divide" mentioned above, as well as discussion and practice of necessary skills, such as research, reading, and writing. Both professors and students express frustration over the expectation of the modes of reading and writing specific to the study of theology–faculty identify a gap in the students' ability, and students feel ill-equipped to learn these modes and perform at the graduate level without sufficient guidance. Such a boot camp could introduce students to the modes of reading and writing that faculty expect and give them space to practice and understand, if not master, these mechanics. Not only would a boot camp provide a vital introduction for students, but it would serve as an understood common starting place for faculty's expectations. Instead of being uncertain regarding students' background abilities and knowledge, faculty would be assured of at least a base level of common knowledge and skills. Likewise, students would be caught up on the minimum expected and required background knowledge and writing and reading styles particular to the field.

Librarian involvement in such a boot camp would be vital. The information to be taught would need to be collated and structured into manageable, programmable pieces, and librarians' facility at one-shot information literacy sessions and stand-alone workshops gives them a unique ability to design the necessary instruction. Librarians also provide support that is knowledgeable about and in tune with the specific needs of the subject matter and the community, but may be fit to focus on general or more broadly applicable mechanics than subject-specific content.

Reading

Reading in graduate school is its own specialized skill. Depending on genre and purpose, students should be utilizing different methods of reading. But it often seems that no one teaches students what they are or how to do it. Students are overwhelmed with the volume of assigned reading; faculty are frustrated with students' lack of facility with handling texts. Students are expected to be able to read for comprehension, trace an argument, perform a close reading, and critically engage, but many students have not been explicitly taught these skills.

Some faculty members expressed that students are too used to the "teach to the test" style of pedagogy, which is clear about foregrounding expectations, but does not encourage the kind of critical and creative thinking that most graduate programs seek to foster. Faculty recognized that students have difficulty reading to identify the author's thesis and argument, instead simply responding with their own opinion of the topic or a thin assessment of either agreement or dissent without a thorough analysis of the text. Teaching how to do this level of reading is more complex than teaching to the test, but it can still be done in a way that is clear about the methods and expectations. Students' reading should be exploratory and critical and should encourage further questioning and engagement. Rather than merely reading for surface-level understanding in order to parrot back facts or quotes, students should be reading to engage texts' arguments, interrogate their evidence, and analyze the validity of their conclusions. This interaction with the text should go beyond mere reflexive, reflective reaction or opinion of agreement or disagreement, but should engage with the logic and context of the text as well. And, as with everything being discussed here, students must be *taught* this kind of method of engagement.

An additional distinctive challenge for theological education is teaching religion to religious students. When teaching Bible to practicing Christian students, for example, students can be too close or too familiar with the subject matter and therefore have a hard time stepping back and reading without the influence of their preconceived ideas. If they are already familiar with the text and their own idiosyncratic reading, it can be difficult for them to read it a different way, particularly if the desired method of reading is not made clear or demonstrated explicitly. This can be especially true if students approach their graduate religion education from a personally religious point of view with religious goals. Teaching them to read religious or theological texts in an academic manner, *as texts*, on their own terms, can be a challenge–even more so if this expectation is not made explicit.

Some professors and teaching assistants I spoke with found that students were resistant to performing critical readings of biblical texts. They were uncomfortable practicing some of the skills of questioning provenance, perspective, purpose, and authorship, and had a hard time when asked to consider the texts might be saying or doing different things than what they had grown up hearing or what they had assumed previously. This resulted in challenges in class and in paper writing, where there seemed to be a barrier in learning that students ran into and could not get past. The resistance limited their ability to learn and explore various textual possibilities, and thwarted teachers' plans and desires. Again, clear communication of what is expected and how to *do* what is expected is essential for overcoming this challenge. Faculty must be clear about the kind of reading students should be performing, and students should be equipped to perform the reading adequately.

Since the job of librarians is practically synonymous with literacy, teaching the skills of specialized reading should be an obvious fit for librarians' engagement. If librarians can teach people to read as children, then why should academic librarians not have a hand in teaching people to read as graduate students? Reading workshops in conjunction with course readings or assignments could be a good opportunity for librarians to teach the unspoken nuances of reading at the graduate level. Demonstrations of how to read in certain modes could serve as a kind of academic story time, where students are exposed to methods of reading and can experience an expert practicing them first hand. Additionally, having an explicit, step-by-step method outlined and distributed would be an invaluable resource for students first learning how to do a critical reading and being able to practice and recreate it on their own.

Writing

An issue that came up again and again in conversations with both students and faculty was the challenge of writing. Students felt ill-equipped to write in a way consistent with the discipline of religious studies or to write in a theological mode. They often had not received explicit training in skills such as developing a thesis statement, outlining an argument, or using evidence to support an assertion. Students expressed a constant feeling of being behind–that they were always trying to catch up to expectations for writing that they had never been taught. Undergraduate instructors assumed they had been taught skills in high school; graduate instructors assumed they had been taught skills in undergrad.

But few instructors were *actually* teaching these skills at any level. Therefore students end up cobbling together ad hoc writing skills, perpetually satisficing rather than absorbing and mastering the necessary methods of the discipline. The result is faculty disappointed with student products but unwilling or unable to teach the skills they believe students should have already learned. Some faculty I spoke with even admitted that they assign far fewer research papers–or none at all–because of the poor outcomes. They found that students were not prepared to write an academic paper with a thesis and evidence-based argument, but were more familiar with journal- or reflection-type essays. Rather than teach them how to construct a research paper (because where is there space in the semester for that?) they simply have turned to other methods of assessing student learning– either by assigning more reflection-type essays or by encouraging alternative creative projects.

The importance of the research paper in graduate education cannot be understated. The process of formulating a research question, proposing a thesis, constructing an argument, and presenting evidence toward a logical conclusion is the bread and butter of scholarship, and to deny students proper instruction toward this end is nothing short of academic negligence. To neglect the development of graduate students' skill in writing the standard research paper is to disregard their learning and to set them up for future difficulties as they continue work in the academy.

Often I find in the course of instructing students in writing that they are not familiar with the five paragraph essay or other very basic writing and organizational methods. Organization and outlining are completely nebulous processes to them. But when they are presented clearly and explained, it's like a revelation and students feel empowered and capable to construct organized arguments with appropriately sourced evidence. The difference that actual, forthright instruction can make! Students don't know what they don't know, and if we want them to display certain abilities and skills, we must teach them explicitly, or at the very least make plain paths for their learning. There is no virtue in making learning more difficult than it already is, in placing a stumbling block in front of students, in the academic hazing of forcing students to figure things out for themselves.

Again, librarians' penchant for programming can come in handy for developing supplementary workshops to teach students the skills they are expected to know but have not been taught. Because there are already such great demands on time and syllabus space for content in the classroom, it's often not tenable to simultaneously teach the mechanics of writing. Having time outside the classroom that is nevertheless directly connected to class assignments is, I would argue, the most effective means for teaching writing. There is a practical application for the information; students can try concepts directly and put them into practice in a way that feels concrete and useful and results in an actual product.

One method of connecting skills-based instruction with a practical application is to think of the library as laboratory. In the same way courses in the sciences might have two meetings of lecture a week plus a lab component, courses in theology and religion could have a lab portion in which they worked in the library or with a librarian to get writing instruction and apply it to their coursework. If a seminar course required a term paper, the lab could be used to pace the students' work and ensure the quality of students' research questions, thesis statements, and resources. Such a lab would provide support for the research and writing process, mitigating the possibility of last-minute, poor-quality papers as well as providing students with writing skills to use in their future work.

Another ready example of library writing support is the thesis writing workshop course my colleague Bobby Smiley and I have developed for students in the Master of Theological Studies program here at Vanderbilt Divinity School. We team up with the school's designated writing tutor to teach sessions on research questions, thesis statements, literature reviews, outlining, citation management, and writing strategies. (See Appendix 1A for a sample syllabus with the full course schedule.) The first half of the semester is dedicated to demystifying the research and writing process, giving the students clear structure for designing their projects, and providing tools, templates, and skills to empower their work. One unfortunate discovery we have made teaching this class is that often students are learning this valuable information in their last semester of the program. We hear time and time again that students wish they would have known these things earlier. The fact that students receive this explicit instruction so gratefully–if not frustratedly–is proof of the disservice being done to them by continuing to rely on unspoken assumptions about their skills and expectations. Giving explicit instruction about the concepts, mechanics, structure, and process of writing a research project results in increased student confidence and ability and better final results. Nothing is gained by keeping students in the dark about how to write well, and assuming they will figure it out themselves only sets them up for failure.

Shame

The unspoken nature of all of these tacit assumptions results in a culture of shame when it comes to students' academic research skills and abilities. Because they are expected to know things, there is a barrier to actually learning them if they don't. There is not space or encouragement for asking questions and the shame is compounded in that so many students likely have the same concerns and questions but are afraid to share them and so suffer in silence. Students avoid speaking up for fear that they are the only ones who don't know something, perpetuating the façade that everyone is on the same page, resulting in further shame when their work is not up to the faculty's standards. It is a cycle that becomes impossible to break without conscious, intentional, and honest conversations regarding expectations and foundational skills.

Research and learning is a vulnerable process, even for the most seasoned scholars. To start from a position of ignorance requires an attitude of humility, curiosity, and openness that is not typically encouraged in the competitive, individualistic academic environment. To further admit ignorance by asking for help or seeking support or collaboration is seen as weakness. The irony of the resistance of professional learners to pursuing the knowledge they need should not be lost. The double-speak of the educational system–that we encourage students and researchers to learn new things and simultaneously shame them for not already knowing–creates a Catch-22 in which everyone, and all of our work, suffers.

One faculty member I spoke with expressed her sense that there is profound fear and shame in classroom discussion. Students don't speak up in class to ask for clarification for fear of revealing their ignorance to the professor and their peers. By staying quiet, they may relieve themselves of the discomfort of vulnerability, but they also then limit their learning and that of others. Students assume they are the only ones who don't understand and so they remain silent and their work suffers, but often if one student has a question, others do too, and everyone would benefit by the vulnerability of asking. The oppressive layer of shame in the classroom keeps students from taking ownership and responsibility for their education and keeps them from helping themselves and others thrive.

Librarians have a unique role to play in changing the academic culture of shame. Because they often are not faculty or course instructors, librarians tend not to create assignments or assign grades, therefore the library can serve as a lower-stakes, lower-pressure environment for leaning into the vulnerabilities of education. To admit ignorance, particularly when one is expected to know, can be a scary prospect. Librarians can create a safer, more comfortable place to learn. By explicitly valuing as well as modeling honest questions, vulnerability, humility, and intellectual hospitality, librarians can begin to change an academic culture of shame to one of exploration and collaboration.

There are many ways librarians can engage students that can minimize shame and fear. Reference desks in libraries are going out of fashion, in favor of on-call, appointment-based reference consultation services. However, consider the frequency with which students approach a circulation desk apologetically, saying "I'm sorry to bother you," or "Excuse me for interrupting." If an official-looking desk is already a barrier, how much more so would students fear entering the office of a stranger, or jumping through hoops to book an appointment? If the goal is to lessen the fear and the barriers inherent in asking for support, then our first concern should be accessibility. Being available and approachable, and recognizably so, means students will be more likely to actually utilize librarians and their resources.

Educating students about the library and the role of librarians is paramount in achieving a recognizable level of accessibility. When students understand what librarians' jobs entail and what they actually *do*, they become increasingly likely to use library services. Building relationships with students and being present in the course of their program in such a way that they can actually get to know us and our expertise not only lets them know the ways we can help them but also lowers the barrier of approachability. Students are much more likely to visit or book an appointment with someone they know than a complete stranger. In my experience, students who know me personally will seek me out for consultations before they go to my colleagues, even if their area of research is more suited to another librarian's expertise, simply because we have a preexisting relationship and the fear of imposing or of meeting with a stranger is diminished.

Exposing the implicit assumptions and expectations in graduate education goes a long way in ameliorating the shame of the current academic culture. Being upfront and straightforward and bringing hidden things to light creates an environment of transparency and honesty where students can feel safe asking questions and being open and vulnerable, which is a necessary part of the learning process. When students feel comfortable discussing their work, they will be able to ask for the help they need, and it will result in a better product. And when the expectations are clear, and the process forthright, resources and support can be readily identified, asked for, and provided without fear of retribution or shame.

Conclusions

The work of graduate education is already challenging enough without having to also do detective work to uncover the expectations and guidelines for your learning. When expectations are clearly communicated and when students are explicitly equipped with the skills they need to meet those expectations, everyone wins. Students achieve their goals and meet their learning outcomes and faculty receive high-quality products and are successful in their own right. So many of the frustrations we hear from both students and instructors over and over again can be ameliorated through straightforward communication and clear exposition of expectations and assumptions inherent in graduate theology and religion programs.

Librarians have much to offer in the way of elucidating academic processes and standards for the specific disciplines of theology and religious studies. We can facilitate communication between faculty and students from the outset, demonstrate and train students in best practices for vital skills like reading and writing, and, perhaps most importantly, we can model the kind of academic environment where shame is abolished and open inquiry and seeking support are encouraged and fostered in earnest. The position of librarians in the educational milieu of the academy is well-suited to do the essential work of bringing clarity and focus to the goals of theological education and to equip students and faculty for success, and we should use this position to bring what's hidden to light and create the kind of environment where transparency and openness result in rigorous and meaningful scholarship for everyone involved.

Appendix 1A : Thesis Writing and Research Methods Workshop Syllabus

DIV 7996 ❖ DIVINITY LIBRARY, VANDERBILT UNIVERSITY ❖ SPRING 2019
M.T.S. Thesis Writing and Research Methods Workshop
Meeting Time/Date TBD | Divinity School 120

Keegan Osinski	Bobby Smiley	Laine Walters Young
Divinity Library, 215B	Divinity Library, 213	Grad. Dept. Religion
keegan.osinski@Vanderbilt.edu	bobby.smiley@vanderbilt.edu	laine.c.walters.young@vanderbilt.edu

Course Description

This is a zero-credit course designed to guide, help, and offer a collective and collaborative venue for completing the M.T.S. thesis. Combining guided practice and workshopping, DIV 7996 will cover how to design, structure, and draft a thesis, as well as introduce academic research best practices and citation tools. Emphasis is placed on practical exercises and instruction for thesis writers, such as formulating research questions, outlining structure, and building a cogent argument for an extended paper (10K plus words/35 pages or more). Ideally, we would like students to be "buddied" up for the semester with their writing partner serving as their principal workshopping respondent and reviewer. While voluntary, students are *highly encouraged* to attend every session. Through attendance, workshopping is made possible, and community building fostered around the often solitary enterprise of thesis writing.

Course Goals and Learning Objectives

The goals of this course are to:

- Envision, draft, write, and submit a thesis on schedule with stipulated deadlines
- Recognize and accommodate the qualitative and quantitative differences in writing for a thesis
- Organize and structure an extended writing project
- Become familiar with the workshopping process and its protocols, as well as best practices around information

Organization

By the end of the course, you should be able to:

- Formulate research questions appropriate for a thesis project
- Identify, locate, evaluate, and organize sources needed in research
- Design and outline a master's thesis
- Apply the practices of workshopping and helpful peer-criticism for future writing projects

The Intellectual Work of the Course

The scholarly diversity among thesis writers is also reflected in our instructors' research interests (Theological Studies = Keegan, Historical Studies = Bobby, Religion, Psychology, and Culture = Laine; for Biblical Studies, Chris Benda will be available). As such, we've collectively marshalled knowledge about citation conventions, key resources, and methodological questions from most research areas in religion, and hope we'll be able to direct and equip you with the resources and perspectives to help you envision and frame the research questions unique to (or more frequently posed in) your area of focus. As part of that process, we will explore how to build out the writerly architecture of master's thesis, and learn about the analytical components for constructing academic arguments and techniques for positing cogent and well-formulated theses.

Suggested Readings

We will be using selections from the following texts:

- Belcher, Wendy Laura. *Writing Your Journal Article in 12 Weeks: A Guide to Academic Publishing Success.* 1st Edition. New York: SAGE Publications, Inc, 2009.*
- Abbott, Andrew. *Digital Paper: A Manual for Research Afterword: Writing for the Public.* Chicago: University of Chicago Press, 2014.†
- Blair, Ann M. "Information overload, the early years," *The Boston Globe.* November 28, 2010.‡

Additional miscellaneous readings and handouts will be distributed in class, or made available electronically.

* This book is *highly* recommended but not required for purchase. A pricey volume, it runs $50 used on Amazon, or anything north of $65 new. It is,

however, a very useful workbook for coaxing you along the writing process.. A copy will be made available on print reserve in the Divinity Library

† This title will also be made available on print reserve in the Divinity Library. Portions of the text may distributed for in-class or assigned recommended reading.

‡ There's the full version of Blair's argument that's well worth reading, which is available as an ebook. See Blair, Ann M. *Too Much To Know: Managing Scholarly Information before the Modern Age.* New Haven: Yale University Press. 2010

Course Calendar

date & topic	agenda & suggested readings	what to bring
Tuesday 1/8 *Introduction to the course*	Introductions & Syllabus **Writing buddy**	Ideas & Questions!
Tuesday 1/15 *Research Qs & theses*	Research questions Abbot, 64-71 How to not jump to the thesis statement **Possible workshopping**	Preliminary research questions & thesis statements
Tuesday 1/22 *Arguments & Outlines*	Making a good argument & Outlines Belcher, 82-92 Summary of *The Craft of Research* (on BrightSpace) **In-class outlining**	Preliminary outlines
Tuesday 1/29 *Peer feedback: proposals*	Proposals for peer feedback (think pair/share) Abbot, 77-85 **PROPOSALS (THESIS, OUTLINE, WORKING BIBLIOGRAPHY) DUE FRIDAY, FEB 1**	Preliminary proposals & preliminary bibliography
Tuesday 2/5 *Literature review:* *Source finding*	Source finding & Managing research Blair, "Information overload, the early years" (online) **Zotero**	Working bibliography
Tuesday 2/12 *Literature review:* *Source reading*	Strategies for reading Belcher, Week 5 Abbott, Chapters 6 & 7	Preliminary literature review
Tuesday 2/19 *Structure & argument*	Strengthening your structure Belcher, Week 6	Outline

Tuesday 2/26 *Literature review:* *Source Finding*	Belcher, Week 7	
Tuesday 3/5 **SPRING BREAK!**	**Time to write!**	
Tuesday 3/12 *Editing & feedback*	Getting, giving, using peer feedback Belcher, Week 9	**FIRST DRAFT**
Tuesday 3/19 *Peer editing*	**Workshopping** **New buddy(?)**	**FULL DRAFT** **DUE MONDAY** **MARCH 25**
Tuesday 3/26 **NO CLASS!**	**Await feedback!**	
Tuesday 4/2 *Individual meetings* **NO CLASS!**	***FACULTY FEEDBACK*** ***RECEIVED BY FRIDAY APRIL 5***	Draft
Tuesday 4/9 *Editing & feedback:* *The sequel*	Faculty feedback & incorporating edit/ suggestions Belcher, Weeks 10, 11	Draft & faculty comments
Tuesday 4/16 *Editing & feedback:* *The finale!*	Final Edits **FINAL DRAFT DUE FRIDAY,** **APRIL 19**	Almost final draft
Tuesday 4/23 **LAST DAY OF CLASSES!**	Drinks? Food? Fun!	

Course Policies

Contacting the Instructors

Please refer the email addresses on the first page of the syllabus for contacting us electronically.

Course Technologies

A laptop computer will be required for all workshopping sessions. A limited number of library laptops are available for checkout, and our classroom may have laptops available as needed. This course will also use Brightspace to post suggested readings, handouts, as well as the syllabus.

Attendance

Attendance for all class meetings is *highly encouraged*, but voluntary. Consistent attendance will afford you the best opportunity to draft and develop your thesis paper in a collective and collaborative environment.

Ethics and Academic Integrity

The Vanderbilt Honor Code applies to all student generated work. Please consult the Code for a more
fulsome explanation of the Honor system, as well as examples of its violation: https://www.vanderbilt.edu/student_handbook/the−honor−system

Special Needs and Accommodations

All accommodations for students with documented needs will need to arrange those accommodations through the Equal Opportunity, Affirmative Action, and Disability Services (EAD). For information, please contact EAD directly: https://vanderbilt.edu/ead/disability_services/contact_us.php

Caveat Emptor

This is a piloted course (and only the second time offered, no less!), and therefore much of the foregoing is open for change. We'll work with you to switch sequencing or refocus emphases if needed. Your feedback throughout the course is very much welcomed and encouraged.

Syllabus Acknowledgments

Special thanks to Wendy Belcher, who generously furnished multiple iterations of her syllabi for *Writing Your Journal Article in 12 Weeks* courses.

CHAPTER 2

Making Our Information Ecosystem Explicit

EVAN KUEHN, TRINITY INTERNATIONAL UNIVERSITY

A LTHOUGH CONVERSATIONS ABOUT INFORMATION LITERACY HAVE GROWN substantially since the ACRL *Competency Standards* (2000) and the *Framework for Information Literacy for Higher Education* (2016) were introduced, a significant amount of fuzzy concept use remains concerning certain information literacy ideas. Sometimes this fuzziness is the result of intentional omission, because the *Framework* and other official documents seek to give as much latitude as possible for developing information literacy instruction relevant to particular communities. This demonstrates a healthy level of flexibility. Elsewhere, however, definitions of concepts circulate among librarians that are problematically inexplicit. In this essay I will discuss one such inexplicit concept–the "information ecosystem"–and offer considerations for how to understand information ecosystems that are local to theological and religious studies disciplines.

The theoretical concern that underlies my argument in this essay can be seen as similar to that posed in a classic text of literacy education, E. D. Hirsch's 1988 book *Cultural Literacy: What Every American Should Know.*[1] Hirsch famously (many would say infamously) argued against what he called "educational formalism," an approach to learning that saw literacy as a skill or technique, which could be taught without reference to any particular content. Hirsch countered this approach to literacy by arguing that literacy always has a context and a large amount of background knowledge to which it constantly refers. In teaching childhood education, then, a reservoir of basic cultural knowledge is necessary for the development of basic literacy skills. I will argue that, in the same way, information literacy cannot be taught without reference to specific background content from which disciplinary researchers build their fluency. The "information ecosystem" is that content-laden context. Making our information ecosystem explicit should, then, be an initial task in preparing for information literacy instruction.

What is an Information Ecosystem?

An information-literate researcher, like any literate person, is literate in some communicative system. For information literacy that system has been dubbed the "information ecosystem." What an information ecosystem is, exactly, is less clear. One might infer that this jargon refers to the library itself, or the scholarly community writ large, but often information ecosystems are described in a way that implies an even more ambitious scope. In the literature, information literacy is also often tied to digital literacy and media literacy because these terms identify where the volume of new information creation is growing most rapidly. Here the information ecosystem is defined in a way that is format-dependent, in an attempt to identify and keep pace with technological developments relevant for research.

Elsewhere, however, the information ecosystem has been defined in terms of research methodology in a way that can obscure its purpose of referring to a field-specific system of information. In keeping with advances into new digital environments, information literacy has been redefined as a "metaliteracy," or a reflexivity about one's creation and use of information.[2] What sort of information ecosystem does the metaliterate researcher engage with? While proponents of the metaliteracy concept (such as *Framework* advocates) continue to associate it with the information ecosystem concept, the idea of an encompassing literacy across information formats distinguished by its self-critical nature does not seem to leave room for any actual system of information in which to claim fluency.[3] Metacognition is surely an important aspect of critical thinking and research, but its very self-referentiality means that it is not meant to refer to any particular field of information, and this seems to exclude it from being a kind of literacy, properly speaking. Reflexive modes of research may be one aspect of information literacy, then, but they cannot be simply synonymous with it.

These concerns at the periphery of information literacy discourse highlight the fuzzy nature of the information ecosystem concept, but the concept itself does seem to be important. The *Framework for Information Literacy* describes a changing information ecosystem for which students and teachers require literacy. This ecosystem was recognized in communications about the *Framework* during its drafting phase, when the ACRL asserted that "since the publication of the first standards, the information environment has evolved into a fragmented, complex information ecosystem that demands greater sense-making and metacognition from the student."[4] Language of the information ecosystem as something to be reckoned with was also retained in the final version of the *Framework*: "the rapidly changing higher education environment, along with the dynamic and often uncertain information ecosystem in which all of us work and live, require new attention to be focused on foundational ideas about that ecosystem."[5] If it is the case that researchers are uncertain about the nature of the information ecosystem in which they pursue their work, then attention to what is foundational about this ecosystem is warranted.

While the *Framework* emphasizes the complex and changing nature of the information ecosystem (in the singular), the IFLA Trend Report *Riding the Waves or Caught in the Tide? Navigating the Evolving Information Environment* offers a more detailed picture of what this ecosystem looks like in relation to the mission of libraries. Noting that "the amount of new digital content created in 2011 amounts to several million times that contained in all books ever written," the report asserts that "how libraries evolve to remain relevant in the new information landscape is perhaps the most urgent question facing the profession today."[6] There is a latent normative assumption in statements like this: vast information content is a matter of relevance and urgency for libraries. At the very least this report implies that libraries are responsible for learning to engage with a new information context that dwarfs all past published print research. At most, it may even imply that libraries have a duty to preserve this content, organize it, and make it accessible to users because it is relevant to their research.

But how relevant is this global information ecosystem–measured in zettabytes of anonymous, corporate, recreational, or repetitive information–to any given academic research library, much less a small seminary library? As Sheila Anderson and Tobias Blanke have noted in their work on research infrastructures for digital humanities, "the humanities do not, and are unlikely to produce large volumes of digital data equivalent to the Large Hadron Collider."[7] Even where information forms a vast and research-relevant ecosystem, it is more likely relevant for the natural or social sciences than for the humanities. Humanities librarians, and religious studies librarians in particular, need not simply accept programmatic statements that identify a radical departure from past practices as obvious existential threats to the relevance of libraries.

From Information Manifold to Information Ecosystem

The massive output of new worldwide information *encompasses* the content that might become a genuine, functioning system of information but as it stands it isn't properly a system in its own right. The information ecosystem as it is portrayed in trend reports or similar forecasting documents (including the *Framework*) is singular, universal, and formidably complex. This idea of the information ecosystem is not, however, actually recognizable in the experience of researchers. To borrow a Kantian term, the information ecosystem as it is usually described is actually more like a "manifold" of information, meaning that it is simply the infinitely diverse array of phenomena that are given to us.[8] This manifold can be synthesized in a way that functions rationally, and I would argue that at this point we have an information ecosystem to speak of–or, more accurately, a pluralism of interrelated information ecosystems. But an information ecosystem isn't just out there in the wild. It is always artificial and therefore needs to be constructed, or at least to emerge from human processes of organization.

Timothy B. Norris and Todd Suomela have recently emphasized this artificial nature of information ecosystems and questioned whether using the ecosystem metaphor for describing systems of information related to scholarly discourse is advisable at all.[9] They critique the metaphor for unduly naturalizing human communication and data itself and for ignoring the natural environmental impact of information economies. Norris and Suomela therefore propose that "information economy" would be a more appropriate way of describing the systems of information and communication that form that landscape of scholarly research. These critiques are well-taken and, while I will continue to use the term "information ecosystem" in this chapter, I do hope to move beyond its under-theorized current state. Information ecosystems are not simply the sum total of all information; this is an overwhelming idea that has little relevance for any individual researcher or research institution. Rather, information ecosystems have functional characteristics related to the disciplinary and subdisciplinary work of the researcher.

Information ecosystems, insofar as they actually function as systems, are more local and diversified than the *Framework* implies. It is true that information ecosystems are usually formidably complex, and so the above-cited reports are correct to point librarians toward the important task of creating infrastructures for research and instruction for research literacy that are a good match for the massive expansion of information today.[10] But in order for the information ecosystem model to be serviceable for subject-specific information literacy, it needs to be defined more explicitly.

Ecosystems can arise from any number of organizing principles. For instance, an information ecosystem could be defined by the network of information updates surrounding a natural disaster or conflict zone. Organizations like Airwars (*airwars.org*) monitor and compile civilian casualty information from four ongoing conflicts, archiving incidents and publishing both reports and social media updates. Airwars incorporates information from Arabic language news sources and social media, NGO and governmental statements, military statistics, and even propaganda sources to identify and corroborate casualties. They also draw on geopolitical and mapping expertise and coordinate with other transparency groups with similar mandates. The emerging field of crisis informatics seeks to define information ecosystems in the sorts of situations that Airwars focuses on and to improve their quality based on analysis of current communication practices.[11] Crises like these offer good examples of how information ecosystems can be complex and widespread but still quite circumscribed by a particular organizational logic. The information ecosystem monitored and contributed to by Airwars is definitely explicit, even if it is emergent and constantly shifting. A similarly complex temporal dynamic has been modeled for natural disaster incidents.[12] In many ways, the goals of crisis-related information ecosystems correspond with the academic librarian's goals of information literacy, albeit under more distressed circumstances. Within the scope of a particular realm of knowledge production, we are concerned with providing researchers an entry into the complexities of communication and interpretation of data, so that these researchers can be responsible consumers of and contributors to human knowledge.

Nancy Foasberg has noted that while the earlier *Information Literacy Competency Standards* (2000) identified academic disciplines as important organizing structures for knowledge, the *Framework* goes as far as to say that "[disciplines] govern the production of knowledge. Disciplinary norms establish which kinds of information are valuable, which directions inquiry can take, and how conclusions can be drawn and supported."[13] Another way of saying this is that disciplinary communities make an information manifold into a genuine ecosystem where information is recognizable, organizable, and usable by the researcher.

Theological and religious studies librarians will be dealing primarily with information literacy instruction grounded in ecosystems of sources that are formed from academic disciplinary communication in theological, biblical studies, and religious studies fields. Before information literacy instruction can begin, theological librarians need to think about learning outcomes in terms of fluency within a particular discourse context. How is theologically relevant information present as an ecosystem? What does fluency in this disciplinary (or subdisciplinary) ecosystem look like? Following are two examples of information ecosystems that librarians may encounter in their work. I have chosen these examples because they are grounded in relatively distinct information systems that present the researcher with complexities beyond basic content considerations such as primary and secondary sources, monographic and serial publication formats, etc.

Information Ecosystem Example 1: Canon Law

The fundamental components of the information ecosystem of theological and biblical studies researchers, and to a large extent of religious studies researchers more generally, are traditional textual modes of communications. These include sacred texts, commentary literature, confessional and canonical documents related to the establishment of community boundaries, as well as a less standardized array of homiletical and devotional literature. Even at this traditional level of the information ecosystem, we encounter complexities that are relevant to information literacy training.

Take canonical documents as an example. The Western Christian canon law tradition begins with an assortment of early writings, gathered into what is known as the *Apostolic Constitutions,* as well as a larger tradition of Roman secular law. In the early and high middle ages these sources and others that had been established over the intervening centuries were gathered and standardized in works such as the *Corpus Juris Civilis* of Justinian I (6th century CE) and Gratian's *Concordance of Discordant Canons* (12th century CE). Collections of canon law and legal commentaries on the Justinian and Gratian collections continued through the medieval and early modern period and were eventually modernized with the 1917 Code of Canon Law and the 1983 Code of Canon Law.

This is an abbreviated summary of two millennia of primary source documents related to an important but easily circumscribed subfield of theological and historical research. Much of this literature is available as affordable or open access translated texts, and these translated versions may be the extent of engagement that undergraduate or even seminary students have with canon law, if they have any at all.[14] Apart from primary text translations, however, critical editions of texts and the manuscript versions upon which they are based offer further layers of complexity. Again, many of these texts are digitized and available online, for instance through the *Carolingian Canon Law*

Project of the University of Kentucky, or the *Medieval Canon Law Virtual Library* run by David Freidenreich of Colby College. [15]

The secondary literature on canon law presents another layer of the information ecosystem. Journals such as *The Jurist* are explicitly devoted to Roman Catholic canon law while others, such as *Ephemerides Theologicae Lovanienses* publish on a range of topics including but not limited to canon law. Meanwhile, journals on religious law like *The Ecclesiastical Law Journal* and *Zeitschrift für evangelisches Kirchenrecht* publish ecumenical and interreligious topics that are nonetheless relevant to the information ecosystem of studies in canon law. Research is coordinated within different interdisciplinary contexts as well. The field of medieval canon law is significant largely because of the above-mentioned work on manuscript evidence and as a key inquiry for establishing a genealogy of modern legal concepts such as human rights or representation. On the other hand, scholars like Norman Doe or Judith Hahn have done significant work on contemporary church law in an intercultural context. [16] These studies can perform similar functions insofar as they offer a "concordance of discordant canons" in their own sense, but they are working with a very different set of texts and ecclesiastical situations.

The information ecosystem relevant for the canon law researcher is relatively traditional: almost wholly text-based and requiring distinctions between primary and secondary sources, manuscripts, print editions both critical and non-critical, historical and constructive work, and journal literature and monographic studies, among other formats. Like most religious studies disciplines and the humanities more generally, the canon law literature is migrating to a digital environment, offering new options for instruction, collaboration, and dissemination of information. These new developments also present challenges for the researcher, as digital projects in canon law are fragmented and require knowledge of a number of different important research hubs without any comprehensive federated search option. Again, this is representative of the digital humanities environment more generally.

Information Ecosystem Example 2: Ethnographic Theology

While the canon law literature may have some unique characteristics, it is representative of most theological fields of study and how their information ecosystems function. There may be a spectrum of textuality among subfields: philosophical theology, for instance, will be entirely textual in nature, while fields like biblical studies or liturgical studies may engage with religious material culture on some level. These fields will include non-traditional and non-text objects as a regular part of their information ecosystem. But even in these cases, the textual and published nature of the information ecosystem predominates. Where unpublished manuscripts are consulted, the published critical edition or published translations are also often considered when available.

Ethnographic research methods are more often employed in non-theological religious studies fields like the anthropology and sociology of religion, although theologians are increasingly engaging with ethnographic research and, in doing so, they are incorporating new objects into the theological information ecosystem. These emerging research methodologies in turn affect the nature of researchers' literacy in sources of theological information. They are less dominated by textual information and require an attention to the difference in structure of their information ecosystem. Natalie Wigg-Stevenson offers a highly attuned account of these differing structures in *Ethnographic Theology*, which analyzes loci of theological research in light of structured interactions and observations in an adult education class that she leads at a Baptist congregation.[17] Robert Orsi's *History and Presence*[18] is another example of religious studies research that draws from ethnographic fieldwork (in this case a vast array of engagements, including pilgrims, interviews with sex abuse victims, religious comics, and autobiography) in order to contribute to theological knowledge about philosophical concepts like presence, transcendence, and history.

Christian Scharen and Aana Marie Vigen describe the information ecosystem relevant for ethnographic approaches to theology in terms of "triangulating data," a common methodological concept in the social sciences that seeks to reinforce the validity of research by employing multiple kinds of data, theoretical models, or data collection methodologies:

> In general, the rule of triangulating data is important to consider. This means one has at least three overlapping but distinct angles of vision on a given project, each offered by virtue of a different method (interviews, observation, participation, document analysis). It also means that as a whole, a research endeavor often relates ethnographic data to relevant quantitative sources of information (e.g., Census data, health/healthcare statistics, poverty indexes, historical documents or narratives of a community, nation, or place). Resourcing quantitative sources of information can help to contextualize what one hears and sees through ethnographic study.[19]

Triangulation of data serves to create an information ecosystem from the cultural manifold that is robust and conducive to researchers' work. Like literacy in any "language," the meaningful cultural formations captured in ethnographic research are always emergent and novel. Facility in their use means one has the ability to orient oneself within new constellations of knowledge and to respond meaningfully to them. A diversified information ecosystem like this may include observed ritual practices, lay description of religiosity conveyed in interviews, folk art depicting biblical episodes, or prayer cards. This is theological information that forms a meaningful system for ethnographic research, although it may be completely irrelevant to more traditional scholastic modes of dogmatic or historical theological research.

Ethnographic theological research is performed in many theological disciplines, from practical theology and ethics to anthropology of religion and missiology. For seminaries that don't tend to focus on social scientific studies of religion, the place where ethnographic work is most prominent may actually be in an MDiv or DMin program, where field research on congregations or clergy is conducted. These programs have different research goals than non-professional theological research programs, and information literacy instruction will need to reflect these different goals. A key indicator for the particular needs of these researchers will be the information ecosystem that can be identified as grounding their theological knowledge production.

Practical Considerations

Although there are basic principles of information literacy that cross disciplines, it is also important to keep in mind that literacy is always facility within a particular context and the wide world of "information" in and of itself is rarely the actual discourse context for which researchers are gaining literacy. With the exception of data scientists themselves, most researchers are a part of a subject-specific ecosystem, or an interdisciplinary range of partially overlapping systems, that remains ordered by the research concerns of a home discipline. In order to use the ACRL *Framework* or other tools for information literacy instruction effectively, instructional and subject librarians need to make their information ecosystem explicit, first for themselves, and also in an ongoing way as they engage with researchers.

The information ecosystem relevant to theological librarianship is multifaceted and requires flexibility and attunement to the research community on the part of the librarian. Before instructing in a classroom setting, it can be helpful to consult with the instructor and/or syllabus to learn what assignments the students will be researching and during instruction to ask them what topics they have chosen for these assignments. In graduate student instruction and especially in a workshop context where attendees are not necessarily following a particular syllabus, reserving time at the beginning of instruction to have students share about their research projects provides a similar opportunity to teach according to the information context of the researchers. During instruction, using examples from the literature related to their topics will help to model a more information-literate understanding of the ecosystem that researchers are entering into. The challenge of this off-the-cuff reference to research literature is that it requires significant familiarity with various theological and religious studies fields in the first place.[20] Not all instructors will be in a position to improvise in relation to these knowledge contexts to the same degree, but even a basic familiarity with the research process of the subfields most relevant to one's institution is important and should be an ongoing priority for theological librarians.

My argument for a more explicit and circumscribed understanding of the information ecosystems relevant for theology and religious studies librarianship should not be taken as the full or final word about the purposes of information literacy as they relate to particular fields of study. It remains true that information literacy is "learning about learning" and that its relevance for lifelong learning and even school learning in liberal arts settings means that information literacy aims at something broader than simply disciplinary content competence. At the same time, theological librarians have a specific task relevant to academic religious studies discourses that is ill-served by fuzzy concept use and a capacious definition of the information ecosystem in the thrall of big data. Information literacy is literacy that is context-specific.

Bibliography

Association of College and Research Libraries. *Framework for Information Literacy for Higher Education.* Chicago: American Library Association, 2016.

Anderson, Sheila and Tobias Blanke. "Taking the Long View: From E-Science Humanities to Humanities Digital Ecosystems." *Historical Social Research / Historische Sozialforschung* 37, no. 3 (141) (2012): 147–64.

Anderson, Sheila. "What Are Research Infrastructures?" *International Journal of Humanities and Arts Computing* 7, no. 1 (2013): 4–23.

Code of Canon Law. Washington D.C.: Canon Law Society of America, 1983.

Crepin-Leblond, Olivier, Anriette Esterhuysen, Divina Frau-Meigs, Melissa Gregg, and John Houghton. *Riding the Waves or Caught in the Tide? Navigating the Evolving Information Environment.* (n.d.). *https://trends.ifla.org/files/trends /assets/insights-from-the-ifla-trend-report_v3.pdf.*

Doe, Norman. *Christian Law: Contemporary Principles*. Cambridge: Cambridge University Press, 2015.

Foasberg, Nancy. "From Standards to Frameworks for IL: How the ACRL Framework Addresses Critiques of the Standards." *Portal: Libraries and the Academy* 15, no. 4 (2015): 699–717.

Fulkerson, D. M., S. A. Ariew, and T. E. Jacobson. "Revisiting Metacognition and Metaliteracy in the ACRL Framework." *Communications in Information Literacy*, 11, no. 1 (2017): 21–41.

Gilchrist, J. T., ed. *The Collection in Seventy-Four Titles: A Canon Law Manual of the Gregorian Reform*. Toronto: Pontifical Institute of Mediaeval Studies, 1980.

Gratianus and Augustine Thompson. *The Treatise on Laws: Decretum DD, 1 - 20*. Washington, DC: Catholic University of America Press, 1993.

Hahn, Judith. *Church Law in Modernity: Toward a Theory of Canon Law Between Nature and Culture*. Cambridge: Cambridge University Press, 2019.

Hirsch, E. D. *Cultural Literacy: What Every American Should Know*. New York: Vintage, 1988.

Kant, Immanuel. *Critique of Pure Reason*, edited and translated by Paul Guyer and Allen W. Wood. Cambridge: Cambridge University Press, 1998.

Kuehn, Evan F. "Reference, Reading, and Nonreading: Learning from Bayard (with a Grain of Salt)." *College and Research Libraries News* 78, no. 10 (2017). *https://doi.org/10.5860/crln.78.10.546*.

Lopatovska, Irene and Bobby Smiley. "Proposed Model of Information Behaviour in Crisis: The Case of Hurricane Sandy." *Information Research* 19, no. 1 (2014). Paper 610. *http://informationr.net/ir/19-1/paper610.html*.

Mackey, Thomas P. and Trudi E. Jacobson. *Metaliteracy: Reinventing Information Literacy to Empower Learners*. Chicago: ALA Neal-Schuman, 2014.

Malenfant, Kara. "ACRL Seeks Feedback on Draft Framework for Information Literacy for Higher Education." *ACRL Insider* (February 20, 2014). *https://www.acrl.ala.org/acrlinsider/archives/8329*.

Norris, Timothy B. and Todd Suomela. "Information in the Ecosystem: Against the 'Information Ecosystem.'" *First Monday* 22, no. 9 (2017). *https://doi.org/10.5210/fm.v22i9.6847*.

Orsi, Robert. *History and Presence*. Cambridge, MA: Harvard University Press, 2016.

Scharen, Christian and Aana Marie Vigen. "Benedictions: For Those Willing to Give Ethnography a Try." In *Ethnography as Christian Theology and Ethics*, edited by Christian Scharen and Aana Marie Vigen, 227–38. London; New York: Continuum, 2011.

Starbird, Kate, Ahmer Arif, Tom Wilson, Katherine Van Koevering, Katya Yefimova, and Daniel Scarnecchia. "Ecosystem or Echo-System? Exploring

Content Sharing across Alternative Media Domains." *Proceedings of the Twelfth International AAAI Conference on Web and Social Media* (2018): 365–74.

Suominen, Vesa. *About and on Behalf of Scriptum Est: The Literary, Bibliographic, and Educational Rationality Sui Generis of the Library and Librarianship on the Top of What Literature Has Produced.* Oulu, Finland: University of Oulu, 2016.

Watson, Alan, trans. *The Digest of Justinian.* 3 vols. Philadelphia, PA: University of Pennsylvania Press, 2009.

Wigg-Steveneson, Natalie. *Ethnographic Theology: An Inquiry into the Production of Theological Knowledge.* New York: Palgrave Macmillan, 2014.

Notes

1. E. D. Hirsch, *Cultural Literacy: What Every American Should Know* (New York: Vintage, 1988).

2. Thomas P. Mackey and Trudi E. Jacobson, *Metaliteracy: Reinventing Information Literacy to Empower Learners* (Chicago: ALA Neal-Schuman, 2014).

3. See the references to the ACRL *Framework* drafts in D. M. Fulkerson, S. A. Ariew, and T. E. Jacobson. "Revisiting Metacognition and Metaliteracy in the ACRL Framework," *Communications in Information Literacy* 11, no. 1 (2017): 21–41.

4. Kara Malenfant, "ACRL Seeks Feedback on Draft Framework for Information Literacy for Higher Education," *ACRL Insider* (February 20, 2014), *https://www.acrl.ala.org/acrlinsider/archives/8329.*

5. Association of College and Research Libraries, *Framework for Information Literacy for Higher Education* (Chicago: American Library Association, 2016).

6. Olivier Crepin-Leblond et al., *Riding the Waves or Caught in the Tide? Navigating the Evolving Information Environment* (n.d.), *https://trends.ifla.org/files/trends/assets/insights-from-the-ifla-trend-report_v3.pdf*

7. Crepin-Leblond et al.

8. Immanuel Kant, *Critique of Pure Reason*, ed. and trans. Paul Guyer and Allen W. Wood (Cambridge: Cambridge University Press, 1998), A77–78/B102–103. What I have described here in Kantian terms is similar to Vesa Suominen's concept of the *Scriptum Est*, or "what literature has produced," which is the basis for the rationality of the library. Indeed Suominen even describes the theoretical question that animates his study as a quasi-Kantian one. Vesa Suominen, *About and on Behalf of Scriptum Est: The Literary, Bibliographic, and Educational Rationality Sui Generis of the Library and Librarianship on the Top of What Literature Has Produced* (Oulu, Finland: University of Oulu, 2016).

9. Timothy B. Norris and Todd Suomela, "Information in the Ecosystem: Against the 'Information Ecosystem,'" *First Monday* 22, no. 9 (September 1, 2017), *https://doi.org/10.5210/fm.v22i9.6847*.

10. See Sheila Anderson, "What Are Research Infrastructures?" *International Journal of Humanities and Arts Computing* 7, no. 1 (2013): 4–23.

11. For an example of crisis infomatics employing the concept of the information ecosystem to media sources reporting on the Syrian civil war, see Kate Starbird et al., "Ecosystem or Echo-System? Exploring Content Sharing across Alternative Media Domains," *Proceedings of the Twelfth International AAAI Conference on Web and Social Media* (2018): 365–74.

12. Irene Lopatovska and Bobby Smiley, "Proposed model of information behaviour in crisis: the case of Hurricane Sandy," *Information Research* 19, no. 1 (2014), paper 610, *http://InformationR.net/ir/19–1/paper610.html*.

13. Nancy Foasberg, "From Standards to Frameworks for IL: How the ACRL Framework Addresses Critiques of the Standards," *Portal: Libraries and the Academy* 15, no. 4 (2015): 704–5.

14. See *Code of Canon Law* (Washington D.C.: Canon Law Society of America, 1983); Alan Watson, trans., *The Digest of Justinian,* 3 vols. (Philadelphia, PA: University of Pennsylvania Press, 2009); Gratian, *The Treatise on Laws: Decretum DD, 1 - 20,* ed. Augustine Thompson (Washington, DC: Catholic University of America Press, 1993); J. T. Gilchrist, ed., *The Collection in Seventy-Four Titles: A Canon Law Manual of the Gregorian Reform* (Toronto: Pontifical Institute of Mediaeval Studies, 1980).

15. Carolingian Canon Law Project, *http://ccl.rch.uky.edu*; Medieval Canon Law Virtual Library, *http://web.colby.edu/canonlaw*.

16. Norman Doe, *Christian Law: Contemporary Principles* (Cambridge: Cambridge University Press, 2015); Judith Hahn, *Church Law in Modernity: Toward a Theory of Canon Law Between Nature and Culture* (Cambridge: Cambridge University Press, 2019).

17. Natalie Wigg-Steveneson, *Ethnographic Theology: An Inquiry into the Production of Theological Knowledge* (New York: Palgrave Macmillan, 2014).

18. Robert Orsi, *History and Presence* (Cambridge, MA: Harvard University Press, 2016).

19. Christian Scharen and Aana Marie Vigen, eds., "Benedictions: For Those Willing to Give Ethnography a Try," in *Ethnography as Christian Theology and Ethics* (London; New York: Continuum, 2011), 230.

20. Evan F. Kuehn, "Reference, Reading, and Nonreading: Learning from Bayard (with a Grain of Salt)," *College and Research Libraries News* (2017), *https://crln.acrl.org/index.php/crlnews/article/view/16804.*

CHAPTER 3

Getting Everyone on the Same Page

Critically Re-imagining Library Instruction for Diverse and International Student Populations

KRIS VELDHEER, CATHOLIC THEOLOGICAL UNION

S O A STUDENT WALKS INTO A LIBRARY... WHILE THIS SOUNDS LIKE THE start to an old joke, it is the everyday world for librarians. Every day theological libraries are visited, both physically and virtually, by people who want to use library resources. But who are the people? What are they looking for? What do they know about using the library? The list of questions we could ask about library users is almost endless. Layer on top of these unknowns the movement toward more intentional international programs in theological education and you get a very diverse user community who needs to be served. Further, the intersection between the library and the user is making library instruction a tricky proposition because of the many factors at play in student populations. Some of these factors–race, national origin, language, age, and educational background–just skirt the edges of the diverse students that walk through the library door, to say nothing of those students present in online programs. In this chapter, I will explore why I think theological libraries are still working from a perspective that underserves diverse, and specifically international, student populations, and how this affects information literacy. Then I will explore ways to address this using part of the Association of College and Research Libraries' (ACRL) *Framework for Information Literacy for Higher Education.*[1] Finally, I will close with examples of how I have begun to get everyone on the same page by reframing information literacy.

Reconsidering the Place of the Theological Library

The basic definition of a library from the *Oxford English Dictionary* is, "A place set apart to contain books for reading, study, or reference."[2] Current libraries, theological or otherwise, are much more complex than this definition. At their core, libraries in the West have operated under an established set of norms that has been in place for decades, if not centuries. Shaped by legacies of colonialism and racism, t hese norms include the use of either Library of Congress or the Dewey Decimal System to arrange physical materials and established systems such as interlibrary loan to give and receive materials from other libraries. Even the arrangement of "service points" such as information or circulation desks and the layout of resources and collections follows predictable patterns in most libraries. With the rise of digital collections and the internet, many libraries are turning to common online tools such as LibGuides and discovery services to curate and manage content. But what lies behind these systems? The systems that are often used to organize and manage libraries have their roots in the American or, more broadly, the Western system of education, which is informed by histories of colonialization and authority vested in white supremecy. In summarizing the work of education theorists Mary Stuart, Catherine Lido, and Jessica Morgan on student experience, Avery and Feist remark in their chapter for *The Globalized Library,*

> [a]s an individual has a habitus, so too do institutions, which may be at odds with an individual's. This can lead to significant discrepancies between higher education experiences of the dominant cultural group and minority ethnic students in higher education, particularly in regards to issues surrounding entitlement and a sense of belonging.[3]

Because of existing structures that have evolved, the theological library might be a place set apart, but it is still a part of a greater educational system all of which needs to be reconsidered.

Since theological libraries have been molded in the same form as the institutions they serve, it is highly unlikely that they are going to completely change their classification systems or radically change long-established circulation practices to incorporate other cultural perspectives. However, many libraries have turned to translating library guides and offering library orientations in various languages. Theological libraries have partnered with or established writing centers to offer classes on plagiarism and research skills in order to help international students. Others have embedded librarians in online classrooms to serve as a resource and many libraries have information literacy programs to bridge gaps in understanding. Whatever form or format it takes, theological libraries are working hard at trying to improve the information literacy skills of their students. But is this enough? Christine Pawley writes in 2003 just after the release of the first set of *Information Literacy Competency Standards for Higher Education* were released by the Association of College and Research Libraries,

> But because statements like the ACRL Competency Standards *also refer, in the techno-management tradition, to the need for 'effective and efficient' information access, and lay out the evaluative criteria on the basis of which information should be selected, information literacy also has the capability to produce and sustain a hierarchical system wherein expert authorities determine what counts as 'knowledge'. Such an approach emphasizes control rather than freedom, and a narrowing (as opposed to a broadening) of selection to those sources deemed 'valuable'. Rather than by all citizens, the tendency of this procrustean paradigm is to fit all contingencies to an 'iron bed', the dimensions of which are predefined by a cultural, social and economic elite.*[4]

ACRL replaced the *Competency Standards* with six interconnected core concepts that can be considered threshold concepts. However, as William Badke summarizes, "The *Framework,* not being a set of standards, becomes difficult to conceptualize and challenging to translate into particular information literacy skill-sets, especially when each discipline views the *Framework* differently. It has been criticized as either overly complex or simplistic, as wedded too strongly to disciplinary structures, and as lacking in emphasis for social justice issues, among other things."[5] With both the *Competency Standards* and the *Framework,* what remains are rigid forms of hierarchy and power as described by Pawley and Badke and they affect the work of the library as a place set apart.

Using the Frame Information Creation as a Process to Begin Reimagining Instruction

In many academic libraries, information literacy needs can be vast. Particularly in the case of theological libraries, which tend to be smaller in size and staff, this need feels more acute because not all seminary students have the same educational background or research experience. Add to the mix varied cultural experiences and information literacy quickly becomes overwhelming for librarians. A brief literature search turns up multiple articles and books about information literacy which seem to fall into three broad categories. First, the undergraduate and specifically first-year experience or secondly, some type of discipline-specific library instruction; generally it is much harder to find literature on information literacy with graduate students. The third category is information literacy with international students. In the introduction to *The Globalized Library*, Yelena Luckert and Lindsey Inge Carpenter write,

> [w]hen reflecting on libraries in the United States, we almost never think of them as being international in nature. We view them as 'American' institutions, serving 'American' patrons and our 'American' organizations. But academic libraries, like institutions of higher education at large, are key players in the effort to educate a diverse student body to be globally conscious members of our communities.[6]

Theological education serves a very diverse student body both geographically and culturally. Who makes up our diverse student body? Are we just working with international students, or do we include a larger population of students in theological education from widely different cultural backgrounds regardless of where they were born? I think it is important to understand who our audience is as we work within the *Framework* to provide instruction for them.

The *Framework* states in its introduction, "Librarians have a greater responsibility in identifying core ideas within their own knowledge domain that can extend learning for students, in creating a new cohesive curriculum for information literacy, and in collaborating more extensively with faculty."[7] This statement suggests theological librarians can draw on their own knowledge domain for their information literacy curriculum. To sharpen the focus of information literacy for theological librarians, let's consider it as a social justice issue. In their 2013 work titled, *Information Literacy and Social Justice*, the editors Gregory and Higgins introduce the concept of critical information literacy building on the work of librarians who are applying critical theories to information literacy. They offer the following proposal:

> Therefore, when we apply critical theoretical approaches to our work as librarians, we consider the historical, cultural, social, economic, political and other forces that affect information so that we may explore ways to critique our understanding of reality and disrupt the commonplace; interrogate multiple viewpoints to identify the status quo and marginalized voices; and focus on sociopolitical issues that shape and suppress information in order to take informed action in the world. Furthermore, when we apply critical theory to our teaching practices, we are working to create a critical pedagogy that helps the learner become aware of the forces that have hitherto ruled their lives and especially shaped their consciousness.[8]

While this seems like a tall order for any librarian to follow, let alone a theological librarian in a small library, I think this is a viable approach to begin getting everyone on the same page and start critically rethinking library instruction. Of the six concepts in the *Framework,* the one I use is Information Creation as a Process. In the following paragraphs, I will explain more about this choice and how I have worked with it.

ACRL describes this concept as "Information in any format is produced to convey a message and is shared via a selected delivery method. The iterative processes of researching, creating, revising, and disseminating information vary, and the resulting product reflects these differences."[9] The field of theology and religion creates information. Many degree programs require students to develop a portfolio or thesis project to complete their master's degrees. So students become participants in the information creation process as they work on their degrees. With the information creation process in mind, I work with this threshold concept for two reasons.

First, I work with it because of the latitude it has for accommodating the wide range of information formats which seminary students encounter from printed works on the one hand to electronic resources on the other. Even within those information formats there is a wide range of formats our students must work through. I often see students in my library with print sources scattered around them while they read an article online and look up vocabulary they might not know on the Internet, all at the same time. Whether engaging students in formal information literacy or in casual conversation, I want students to understand that the information they are using was produced to convey a message. Can they identify the message? How does the information they find in a book compare with something they might have found online? How does using a full text article they found online compare to an article in a print journal? Helping students discern subtle contextual cues about information creation helps them in their own information creating process.

Secondly, I use Information Creation as a Process because it indirectly addresses the many issues listed above in the quote from Gregory and Higgins on the forces that affect information. Further, I think this concept brings students closest to what Pawley referred to above as "opening up possibilities for social, cultural, and economic participation in knowledge production."[10] Helping students understand that information just doesn't appear in a finished format but has a creation process then creates a place for them to insert themselves into the material. Students can bring their contexts and experiences into worship resources or search for a Bible commentary from their cultural perspective. I think this picks up on some of the dispositions associated with the threshold concept such as seeking out characteristics of information products and accepting their uncertainty about the value of information creation in emerging formats.[11]

The *Framework* offers other threshold concepts to reimagine library instruction, but it isn't a quick fix. With the sheer amount of information available to students, this isn't an easy task for librarians either. I think by teaching students to see themselves in the information creation process, we can teach them to utilize their own contexts and experiences to understand and use information more effectively. There is also plenty of room to weave in other threshold concepts from the *Framework* as well.

What's Working for Me

One of the most frequent questions I hear when librarians talk about information literacy is "What works for you?" In this closing section, I will give three examples that have worked for me and that I continue to use. In each of these examples, you may be able to layer other threshold concepts that I don't work with as much or that may work better in your context.

The first example is using games to teach concepts like the library research process. In the early 2000s, I used a quiz show-style game with the questions projected on a screen and students would call out the answers. This was easy to prepare and easy to adapt for different research topics. However, it favored bolder students who felt comfortable speaking up in a group or had a better grasp of English. I also experimented with breaking the group in teams of two to three students to encourage both individual and group learning. During that time period, using handheld clickers to encourage student participation was somewhat popular. The preparation was more complicated because the software wasn't always user-friendly and it also required purchasing the clickers. Another disadvantage I discovered to using clickers in games was that it didn't allow me to identify the students who didn't understand the concepts I was teaching. The software aggregated the responses to the quiz questions and, depending on the responses, I could only offer broad explanations and examples to illustrate my point rather than targeting who was still having trouble. The use of games in the classroom can be a welcome change from a regular lecture format and encourages interactive learning. With Information Creation as a Process, gaming can be used to teach the pros and cons of using one source over another, explaining how reference works like encyclopedias are created, and why libraries have more than one edition of a book on a shelf.

In the more than fifteen years since I started working with games there has been a virtual explosion in gaming software and gaming apps. A good source that

I have used to stay current on gaming for the classroom is from the website *Ditch That Textbook* by Matt Miller. He offers a regularly updated analysis of the latest in web-based resources to create a game show classroom.[12] Personally, a colleague has tried Kahoot! (*kahoot.com*) with some success in teaching research skills. Although Kahoot! offers an easy way to get classroom gaming up quickly, there are a couple of drawbacks. First there is no free, anonymous trial. In order to use Kahoot! you must create an account, even for the free version. Second, students need to have loaded the Kahoot! app onto their mobile devices to play along. While neither of these is a deal breaker since most students have some type of mobile device, you will need to build setup time into your classroom schedule to ensure every student can participate in your games. Unfortunately, only the paid versions, Kahoot! Plus and Kahoot! Pro, offer detailed reports on student progress so there isn't a ready way to identify which students may need additional help. There are also many other online packages such as Quizlet which might offer different features more apt for use in your information literacy instruction. The best part of using web-based resources is they are usually easy for the instructor to set up and can be recycled for use in other classes easily.

A second example is identifying the prerequisite or common library research skills that might not be so common to your audience. As Russell and Hensley point out about digital tools, but which I would argue applies to library research skills in general, "One of the most challenging aspects of teaching digital tools is forgetting what it is like to be a novice learner."[13] Let me give you three scenarios from my experience that illustrate this and how I responded. In the first scenario, students from a class walk into the library with a bibliography. The assignment was to find items from the bibliography to read for a class discussion and most students seemed to be finding the items quite quickly. However, one of the international students was struggling to make sense of the bibliography. After a lengthy conversation, I realized the student didn't know how to identify the parts of a citation in order to find articles and books. To remedy this, I included a small-group exercise in library instruction where students are handed a bibliography and need to identify the parts of each citation. Then the bibliography is projected at the front of the room and the groups name the parts of a citation, such as author, title, year of publication and so on. The bibliography used in the game was designed to highlight hard-to-identify items like an essay in an edited work, various ways journals are numbered, and differences in editions. The ulterior motive is to also reinforce the process of how information is created. There is also room here for the novice learner to learn from other students by allowing students to work in lanugage groups such as Spanish-speaking students or Vietnamese students working together around an English-language bibliography.

In the second scenario, it may be sometimes important to understand what a library is where the student comes from. Recently I had a student in the reference stacks ask me about which was better, the first or second editions of a common Bible dictionary. In conversation, the student told me the library at her school in Asia has closed stacks and she is allowed only a few volumes at a time. Further, she said having access to all the books on the shelf in my library was overwhelming. I realized that she may not know the difference between editions and how to compare them. In previous information literacy instruction I have always skirted around this issue, but now I realize that, depending on the audience, I need to make this a deliberate part of future instruction. As a library, we also need to make these seemingly basic library skills part of any online research guides we create, and we need to promote their use to our students. Students may not understand information creation is a process if they only have access to a few books at a time and it is important to provide them with the necessary clues to working in a different library environment.

The third scenario involves the issue of citing sources and avoiding plagiarism. In my institution students are sent to either the library or the writing center for citation help and the library director teaches the plagiarism and citation workshops. I know even students educated in U.S. universities who struggle to make sense of style guides in order to avoid plagiarism. Several years ago while working at another library, I was asked to teach a citations workshop for a group of African students. Without thinking, or considering the citation as a colonial construct, or recognizing what legacies are embedded in our teaching context, I pulled out my standard workshop on citations and began to teach the class. While the students were sitting quietly and nodding as if they understood, only one student was answering my follow-up questions during the session. At the midpoint of the workshop, I stopped teaching and asked them if I was really making sense. Following a prolonged period of silence, one student spoke for the group in telling me no, this made little sense to them. As it turns out, for many of the African students, English was their fourth or fifth language after the colonial language of their country and various tribal languages they spoke. Further, for some their previous education was not concerned with plagiarism or citing sources. In that moment, I realized my whole presentation wasn't going as planned. So, I stopped the presentation, turned off the PowerPoint slides, and began to teach Turabian like math problems because they said they all could do math. By presenting book citations as author + title + city of publication + publisher + year of publication = book citation, I began to teach these students to cite sources. Similar "math equations" were written for journal articles, websites, and the like, until the students had a basic grasp on the elements of a citation and the order in which they needed to go. This was by far a less-than-elegant solution, but one I have found very useful working with students from many backgrounds. It also reminds me to place many checks for understanding in my lesson plans while at the same time not making assumptions about workshop participants and acknowledging the content and consequences of the instructional context, as well as my own positionality as the instructor.

The above scenarios point to only three instances when "common knowledge" or prerequisite skills just weren't present in the students during information literacy instruction. In the past, I would have gone with my assumptions that this applied to mostly international students, but more recently I am seeing the same skills lacking in students educated in the U.S. I have yet to determine if this is due to cultural context, social influences, or the economic circumstances the students are coming from, however these factors can influence how students see information creation as a process. I think that, without the prerequisite skills, students cannot see themselves in the information creation process or see how to use their own stories to create new knowledge. They also cannot make informed choices about which information sources they want to use for their research or understand how using one edition over another may matter in their field of study.

In my final example, I want to take up the old debate among librarians of the "one shot" workshop over longer teaching opportunities as part of the wider school curriculum. Is it realistic to think librarians can cover enough in a workshop or two so students understand Information Creation as a Process or any of the other threshold concepts? Of course, I would answer that librarians never think one shot is enough. However, what can we do with the one shot we may get? I think we can use the "one shot" or any limited opportunity as a gateway to multiple library instruction sessions. At a prior institution, following a conversation in which faculty were lamenting about the quality of student papers, I suggested sessions of library instruction to improve assignment quality. Unfortunately, what I received in return was a single class session when the professor was out of town. Concentrating on improving their research skills, I worked with the students on their next writing assignment to find sources they could include. This wasn't a writing workshop, but rather an opportunity to improve research skills. After the workshop, during a follow-up with the faculty, there was noticeable improvement in the next assignment. While this didn't result in immediate adoption of a wide-ranging information literacy program, it did lay the groundwork for repeated one-shot workshops which could be strung together to teach a variety of information literacy skills over time. Further, it led to creating assignments with faculty that intentionally included developing research and information management skills. By using the gateway approach, I was able to move toward what Powell and Kang refer to as "advocating for an intensive workshop model that gives librarians the space to move beyond solely skills-based learning outcomes to more advanced, situated knowledge."[14]

What I have not covered in my three examples above is the burgeoning world of online programs that theological libraries are required to support. Many theological schools are much further along in this process than others. Just because I didn't choose to highlight that world in the above examples doesn't imply that I take it lightly. Rather, I think online education holds great promise for theological libraries in embedding librarians in online classes and being able to design more detailed self-paced instruction for students. Many librarians in Atla are leading the way on this front and I think it is important to acknowledge their work. Directly and indirectly, any efforts theological librarians make toward critically reimagining their libraries using the *Framework* will improve the scholarship in the field of theological education. It will also inch along the process of challenging and reimagining instruction to be more inclusive of diverse student populations, including international students.

Conclusion

Getting everyone on the same page in the library is a Herculean task given the diversity in theological education. Nonetheless, any time we can use critical theory to break out of existing preconceptions and paradigms, librarians can try to challenge and reconceive library instruction for diverse student populations, one workshop at a time. Given that the *Framework for Information Literacy* lacks an emphasis on social justice issues, it becomes the responsibility of librarians to insert those issues back into their information literacy practices. As a whole, many parts of the *Framework* could help work toward reimagining library instruction and Information Creation as a Process is only one frame. I think when students understand how the information they are working with was created, it unlocks the opportunity for them to see themselves as co-creators of information too. As Russell and Hensley point out, "in other words, we are guiding scholars along the process of learning how to learn."[15]

Bibliography

Arghode, Vishal, Earl W. Brieger, and Gary N. McLean. "Adult Learning Theories: Implications for Online Instruction." *European Journal of Training and Development* 41, no. 7 (2017): 593–609.

Association of College and Research Libraries. *Framework for Information Literacy for Higher Education*. Chicago: American Library Association, 2016.

Avery, Susan and Kirsten Feist. "Unlocking the Door: Adapting Information Literacy Instruction for International Students." In *The Globalized Library*, edited by Yelena Luckert and Lindsey Inge Carpenter. Chicago: Association of College and Research Libraries, 2019.

Badke, William. "DIKTUON: The Framework for Information Literacy and Theological Education: Introduction to the ACRL Framework." *Theological Librarianship* 8, no. 2 (October 2015): 4–7.

Fulkerson, Diane M., Susan Andriette Ariew, and Trudi E. Jacobson. "Revisiting Metacognition and Metaliteracy in the ACRL Framework." *Communications in Information Literacy* 11, no. 1 (2017): 21–41.

Gascho-Rampel, Hannah and Jeanne Davidson. "Providing Information Literacy Instruction to Graduate Students through Literature Review Workshops." *Issues in Science and Technology Librarianship* (Winter 2008). *http://www.istl .org/08-winter/refereed2.html*.

Gregory, Lua and Shana Higgins, eds. *Information Literacy and Social Justice: Radical Professional Praxis*. Sacramento, CA: Library Juice Press, 2013.

——. "Reorienting an Information Literacy Program Toward Social Justice: Mapping the Core Values of Librarianship to the ACRL Framework." *Communications in Information Literacy* 11, no. 1 (2017): 42–54.

Avery, Susan and Kirsten Feist. "Unlocking the Door: Adapting Information Literacy Instruction for International Students." In *The Globalized Library*, edited by Yelena Luckert and Lindsey Inge Carpenter. Chicago: Association of College and Research Libraries, 2019: 19-28.

Moritz, Carolyn, Rachel Smart, Aaron Retteen, Matthew Hunter, Sarah Stanley, Devin Soper, and Micah Vandegrift. "De-centering and Re-centering Digital Scholarship: A Manifesto." *Journal of New Librarianship* 2 (2017): 102–9.

Moten, Abdul Rashid. "Academic Dishonesty and Misconduct: Curbing Plagiarism in the Muslim World." *Intellectual Discourse* 22, no. 2 (2014): 167–89.

Pawley, Christine. "Information Literacy: A Contradictory Coupling." *The Library Quarterly: Information, Community, Policy* 73, no. 4 (October 2003): 422–52.

Powell, Susan and NingNing Nicole Kong. "Beyond the One-Shot: Intensive Workshops as a Platform for Engaging the Library in Digital Humanities." *College & Undergraduate Libraries* 24, no. 2 (2017): 1–16.

Russell, John E. and Merinda Kay Hensley. "Beyond Buttonology: Digital Humanities, Digital Pedagogy, and the ACRL Framework." *College & Research Libraries News* (December 2017): 588–600.

Wood, Gail. "Academic Original Sin: Plagiarism, the Internet, and Librarians." *The Journal of Academic Librarianship* 30, no. 3 (May 2004): 237–42.

Notes

1. Association of College and Research Libraries, *Framework for Information Literacy for Higher Education* (Chicago: American Library Association, 2016).
2. "library, n.1," *OED Online*, accessed 17 March 2019.
3. Susan Avery and Kirsten Feist, "Unlocking the Door: Adapting Information Literacy Instruction for International Students," in *The Globalized Library*, ed. Yelena Luckert and Lindsey Inge Carpenter (Chicago: Association of College and Research Libraries, 2019), 20.
4. Christine Pawley, "Information Literacy: A Contradictory Coupling," *The Library Quarterly: Information, Community, Policy* 73, no. 4 (October 2003), 426–427.
5. William Badke, "DIKTUON: The Framework for Information Literacy and Theological Education: Introduction to the ACRL *Framework*," *Theological Librarianship* 8, no. 2 (December 2015), 4–5.
6. Yelena Luckert and Lindsey Inge Carpenter, eds., *The Globalized Library* (Chicago: The Association of College and Research Libraries, 2019), vii.
7. ACRL, *Framework*, Introduction.
8. Lua Gregory and Shana Higgins, eds., *Information Literacy and Social Justice* (Sacramento, CA: Library Juice Press, 2013), 3.
9. ACRL, *Framework*.
10. Pawley, 426.
11. ACRL, *Framework*, Dispositions.
12. Matt Miller, "Ditch that Textbook," last updated September 2018, *https://bit.ly/29ReqO3*.
13. John E. Russell and Merinda Kaye Hensley, "Beyond Buttonology: Digital Humanities, Digital Pedagogy, and the ACRL Framework," *College & Research Libraries News* (December 2017): 590.
14. Susan Powell and NingNing Nicole Kong, "Beyond the One-Shot: Intensive Workshops as a Platform for Engaging the Library in Digital Humanities," *College & Undergraduate Libraries* 24, no. 2 (2017): 8.
15. Russell and Hensley, 590.

CHAPTER 4

Framing Information Literacy within the Disciplines of Theological Education

WILLIAM BADKE, TRINITY WESTERN UNIVERSITY

THEOLOGICAL EDUCATORS HAVE AGREED FOR DECADES THAT SIMPLY providing a knowledge-based education is inadequate in seminary instruction. Seminaries build scholars who are at the same time practitioners, embodying their knowledge so that they develop expertise and practical abilities to minister to others. While the actual focus of that ministry may vary widely, it is clear that the purpose of seminary is to produce knowledgeable practitioners.[1]

Those who see academic disciplines as embodiments of knowledge miss the point that they are in reality "communities of practice."[2] That is, disciplines are dynamic entities in which a history of interaction over key issues actually forms the content. This is expressed succinctly in the Association of College and Research Libraries' (ACRL) *Framework for Information Literacy in Higher Education* concept, Scholarship as a Conversation.[3] The content of disciplines only exists and thrives in a vital community of disciplinarians who converse to shape it and define its purposes.

Theological educators thus face a potential dilemma: While there is much content to disseminate in courses, disciplines are about practice as much as they are about content. If the goal of theological education is the development of practitioners, then teaching disciplinary practice is essential to the instructional process.[4] Unfortunately, the first barrier for most students lies in the fact that they are not members of the disciplines they are studying. While they may learn enough facts to pass examinations, unless they are enculturated in disciplines, they can remain outsiders to the scholarly conversation that their professors understand well.

Enculturation involves enabling students to become participating citizens in disciplines. Lave and Wenger described such enculturation as "legitimate peripheral participation."[5] It is legitimate in that it has to be an authentic in-discipline experience, not just an imitation of disciplinary activities. It is peripheral, at least at first, because it does not engage the central discipline but works at the edges of it, gradually moving students closer to the center as time goes on. The best analogy is that of a recent immigrant who comes into a country, participates in various activities in common with citizens, and gradually becomes more centrally a citizen in thought and action.

We might ask why theological students even need to engage in enculturation. Most of them come from a faith community and thus understand at least some of the content and conventions of the disciplines they are studying. While this is true, there are inevitable barriers to full participation. It is one thing to have a lay grasp of the details of theological disciplines, but another to be involved in disciplines as practitioners. Theological education, in fact, contributes to development of barriers by setting up professors as experts and students as learners. When we add the peculiar cultures of communities found within disciplines and the rigorous methods practiced in disciplines, we find many students are alienated to a greater or lesser degree as they begin taking courses.

When it comes to information literacy, it is possible to teach students generic research methods, but these methods often fail to help them become full participants in disciplines. Thus, the concept of "situated information literacy" is better positioned to help students become disciplinarians. Situated information literacy argues that the goals of research differ from discipline to discipline and that the only truly viable approach to instruction is to do it within the context of disciplines.[6]

What is a Discipline?

While disciplines may well be described as "communities of practice,"[7] disciplinary culture needs to be viewed as complex and nuanced. Along with my colleague, Robert Farrell,[8] I have argued that disciplinary culture consists of three foundational elements: epistemology, metanarrative, and method.[9]

Epistemology involves the knowledge base of a discipline–how it developed, who the major players are (past and present) and what criteria make one piece of knowledge more authoritative than another. Its closest connection to the *Framework* is the concept, Authority is Constructed and Contextual.[10] Clearly, each discipline has a foundational knowledge that is formed and reshaped by the research done in the discipline. Understanding the nature of that knowledge and of the value placed on it by members of the discipline is a crucial first step in disciplinary understanding. Lambek, for example, has argued this about disciplines: "Each is a tradition of scholarship building upon certain evolving epistemological commitments and judgments."[11] Thus epistemology sees the knowledge base as not only growing but finding its justification in the culture (metanarrative) and methods of the discipline. Disciplinarians take the primary role in assessing the authority of the discipline's knowledge. This is not to say that the epistemology of any discipline is uniform. While there may be mainstream understandings, there are always participants who challenge what a discipline claims to know and the ways in which it evaluates its knowledge (thus affirming that authority is contextual).

Metanarrative, a culture's understanding of the beliefs and norms that shape its story, is at the heart of what we mean by saying that a discipline is a "community of practice."[12] The concept of metanarrative answers questions like: What motivates scholars in this discipline? How varied is their internal culture? Members of a discipline recognize one another and understand one another. They agree to an ethos that defines them as scholars of a subject area and provides them with a cultural sense of how they function as citizens of the discipline. No discipline, however, has a monolithic metanarrative. There may be a broad core understanding but, like any culture, there can be dramatic variants. Recent research has criticized the very notion of disciplinary metanarratives, though it is hard to imagine any discipline without a culture (as varied as it may be) that holds it together.[13] Grasping the nature of a disciplinary culture is key to becoming a member and player in the discipline.

The *Framework* describes metanarrative with Scholarship as a Conversation.[14] That is because scholarship is not an individual but an interactive function, scholar to scholar. Metanarrative also interacts extensively with epistemology (the information we value, based on the mandates of the culture we live in) and with method (which is determined by the cultural mandates of the discipline). We can separate the three modes of disciplines conceptually, but in practice they function together, each informing the other. As a trinity of factors, they enable an ongoing conversation in the discipline around best practices, findings and variant explanations.

Method is the means by which a discipline advances. It is crucial that the research within a discipline be done by means agreed to by disciplinary practitioners, or there is no way to determine the authority of research findings. Students who do research and write outside of recognized norms for the discipline will find themselves contradicted by their professors. This is not to say that there are not voices in every discipline who discount existing methods or suggest even radically new ones. But all methods have to stand up to the test of the academy–that is, to the disciplinary practitioners who pass judgment on what methods will survive and what will be rejected as illegitimate. Method is governed both by epistemology (what information we value and affirm) and by metanarrative (how research methods reflect the ethos and goals of the discipline).[15]

The growing movement of interdisciplinary studies in theological education may seem to contradict the disciplinary themes we have just described. Does an interdisciplinary approach not contradict the very notion of disciplinary cultures and method? No. When scholars from two or more disciplines work together, a new discipline emerges. These scholars come to share a new ethos (built around the values of interdisciplinarity and the disciplinary cultures they come from) and a set of methods they need to agree upon. As they do their work, they also establish a knowledge base. It seems impossible to do genuine scholarly work outside of the environment of disciplinary conventions, even if these have evolved in an interdisciplinary context.

Understanding the Disciplines of Theological Education

Armed with an understanding of the nature of disciplines and informed by relevant concepts in the *Framework,* it is possible to establish a means to understand each discipline and thus to function within its culture and discourse. This is the ultimate goal of any entry of novices into a discipline: to begin thinking, speaking, and researching like the citizens of the culture. Simmons has argued that librarians need to become "disciplinary discourse mediators:"

> *The librarian can teach the … student the ecology of the disciplinary environment, with the subject scholar delving more deeply into one specific discipline's practices. This cooperative approach, involving both the librarian and the scholar in the initiation of … students into a particular discourse community, provides students both a view of the breadth as well as experience with the depth of disciplinary research.*[16]

Librarians need to help develop researchers who can formulate disciplinary-sensitive research questions/theses, locate the highest quality and most relevant resources, identify the scholarly conversations, engage with those conversations, and write like disciplinary citizens.

That may seem like a very tall order. Who are librarians to think that this is a possible, or even desirable, role for them? Is not the introduction of students into disciplines the work of professors? That would be the case if we were seeing consistent signs that students were being successfully enculturated. Yet professors themselves express dismay over the poor levels of student research and the limited quality of student discourse. Christine Wenderoth's interview study with seminary faculty reflects this dilemma: "So, faculty see that students can't do research (and so can't learn from each other the way they did in graduate school, supposedly). Yet, by their own admission, these same faculty are not teaching research to their students, sometimes feeling guilty about that, sometimes just angry."[17]

The seminary world does have two advantages over larger universities. First, seminary librarians, because of accreditation standards, are generally faculty rather than staff. Second, the relatively smaller size of seminaries means that it is possible for librarians to have more significant input into issues related to student disciplinary information literacy.

What follows is an attempt to build a model for disciplinary understanding and information literacy, using the most central seminary disciplines: biblical studies, theology, and pastoral studies. True, there are many more disciplines: counseling, apologetics, justice studies, and so on, but our analysis is not intended to be exhaustive, only to provide examples of ways in which librarians along with faculty can develop a consciousness of the tasks involved in student disciplinary enculturation. With our first discipline, biblical studies, we will do a fairly extensive analysis. Following disciplines will engage the same analytic questions more briefly.

Clearly, each discipline in theological education is complex and multi-faceted. Rather than focusing on a discipline's diversity, we will identify the core elements that define the discipline and then branch out into its varieties. We recognize that, for seminary disciplines, the worldviews of scholars can create significant divergences, yet there are still foundational values and methods that remain.

Biblical Studies as a Discipline

The field of biblical studies has a very long history, going back to intra-biblical interpretation of earlier biblical writings by later ones. Fortunately, we have many published histories of biblical scholarship that provide insight into how we got to today's version of the discipline.[18] In the following analysis, we will ask pointed questions around the three primary elements of biblical studies as a discipline–epistemology, metanarrative, and method–in an attempt to support students as they become enculturated.

Biblical Studies: Epistemology

Question #1—What is the most essential knowledge in the discipline?
For biblical scholars the text is utterly foundational. No biblical scholar, however unconventional, is flippant about the primacy of the biblical text. The text is more foundational to biblical scholars than method or even than metanarrative, both of which arise from the text. As Kenneth Hagen has argued: "If you want to talk about method, be realistic. We begin with the text, the Book. We begin with eyes, hands, minds, questions, issues, goals, and yes, deadlines. The task is study and interpretation. How to read the Book? The best way is to start by reading-slowly."[19]

Further, the text is best informed by the environment out of which it developed, so understanding that environment is crucial. Here, students will need to be introduced to writings of the Ancient Near East, texts of Judaism that are beyond the biblical canon, and all the ancient historical matter that has come down to us from biblical studies. For some scholars, the primary literature under consideration also encompasses the history of the reception of the biblical text through the Fathers, the Scholastics, the Reformers, and beyond.

Secondary sources have their place as well. More on this in answer to the next question.

Question #2—How did the knowledge base develop over time?
This may seem like a simple question requiring us to trace the history of biblical study and arrive at an understanding of the literature the discipline depends upon. The fact is, however, that the history of biblical study is varied and convoluted. Much of it has been shaped by various presuppositions about the text and various theological beliefs. While that is the case, we can explain knowledge base development in a way that, though simplistic, has enough truth in it to make it workable: The knowledge base developed as biblical practitioners over time sifted through all that had been written and then achieved some form of consensus as to what was important. Here we have the work of Church Fathers, Scholastics, Reformers, Biblical criticism pioneers, and modern scholars.

A two-fold caution needs to be raised here: The knowledge base of biblical studies is not uniform nor is it static. This is where epistemology, metanarrative, and method interact vigorously. While there are foundational elements in the biblical literature base, that base is also the product of a wide variety of belief systems (metanarrative) that have used divergent methods to create a landscape that is not nearly as uniform, nor as settled in its content, as a beginning student may think. This is where the idea from the *Framework* that Authority is Constructed and Contextual has particular value.[20] To argue that the accepted knowledge base of biblical studies simply developed by adding one writing after another to it is to miss the point that what survives has been negotiated in the scholarly community so that the authority of any piece of literature is based on having passed tests for authority.[21]

Biblical Studies: Metanarrative
Metanarrative gets at the heart of the culture, belief system, and goals of the discipline. To enter a field of study, understanding its metanarrative is essential to determining how to belong.

Question #1—What motivates biblical scholars?
Most seasoned biblical scholars would point to the biblical text as their motivational core: They want to understand the text in light of... but we must pause here, because this is where the complexity of biblical scholar metanarrative reveals itself. If we were to compare the metanarrative of biblical scholarship to language, we would have to say that there is a central language but several related languages and dialects. It is an often uncomfortable reality that the motivation of each biblical scholar arises out of that scholar's presuppositions, belief system, and vision for the purpose of the text.

The foundational motive of biblical scholarship is exegesis–the reading of meaning from the text. Before scholars can determine what should be done with biblical passages, they need to understand them. Thus, the biblical commentary, and numerous books/articles directly on the exegesis of the biblical text continue to abound. Were we just to look at these products, we might assume that biblical scholarship is simply discourse over understandings of the text. And there would be good reason to believe this, considering the number of references to biblical history, extra-biblical sources, and so on that fill biblical commentaries. Massey Shepherd, somewhat sarcastically, referred to the critical biblical commentary as, "A filing cabinet of possibly helpful clues to a reader."[22] Yet there is much more diversity in biblical studies than beginning students assume. Understanding the text is a foundational value, but that value is complex in its practice.

Question #2—How diverse is the biblical studies metanarrative?
Biblical studies has a quite wide metanarrative. While there are some scholars who doggedly exegete the text, probing its meaning to evoke the message communicated by its original author, most biblical scholarship also recognizes that biblical study is to a greater or lesser extent "critical." That is, there is an assumption that there are few easy answers in biblical scholarship, and the ways in which we view the text, our presuppositions if you will, largely govern the conclusions we make.[23]

If, for example, we consider the Old Testament text to have developed over time, so that many of its books have no single author but were compiled from several sources, or if we challenge the original dating of the books (seeing Deuteronomy as the product of the late pre-exilic era, etc.), this will reshape our face-value interpretations in fairly dramatic ways. For a student entering the world of biblical scholarship, the following simple example is helpful. It relates to the differences between two common books on biblical exegesis, both coming from the same publisher.

Gordon Fee's *New Testament Exegesis: A Handbook for Students and Pastors* focuses on interpreting the biblical text in its historical and cultural context. Fee argues that "exegesis is primarily concerned with intentionality: What did the author *intend* his original readers to understand?"[24] There is no significant reference to alternative methods of exegeting the text. For Fee, the metanarrative of the biblical scholar involves a consuming desire to discover what the presumed author meant in that author's historical-cultural context. Fee's presupposition is that the text needs to be taken more or less at face value, given that genres and the author's ways of understanding text in his day will shape our understanding.

John H. Hayes and Carl R. Holliday, using the same publisher as Fee, present a very different vision of exegesis in their book, *Biblical Exegesis: A Beginner's Handbook.* While they see interpreting the meaning of the biblical text as foundational (the common metanarrative for biblical scholars), their presupposition is that most biblical books "appear to have developed over lesser and greater lengths of time and many persons probably contributed to their formation."[25] With the lack of a concept of a single author and the addition of a long history of text formation, the task of finding meaning takes a turn toward enlisting critical methods that do a broader analysis of the text. Thus, Hayes and Holliday devote most of their book to describing types of criticism that can be enlisted in exegesis–textual, historical, grammatical, literary, form, tradition, redaction, structuralist, and canonical. It is not that finding the meaning of the text is unimportant but that doing so is more complicated than it appears on face value.

The aspirations of biblical scholars vary as well. For some, academic study of the text is enough. For others the text is sacred Scripture so that exegesis naturally leads to application in preaching and teaching. For still others, texts must speak to common social issues like feminism, post-colonialism, social inequality, justice, and so on. In all cases, finding meaning in the text is foundational, but the purposes to which the text and its understanding are to be directed will vary. Basic tools like *The Cambridge Companion to Biblical Interpretation*[26] can form a doorway for students into the main metanarrative versions that guide biblical methods active today.[27]

Biblical Studies: Method

Question #1: What are the standard methods used in biblical studies?
Once we have understood the nature of the epistemology and metanarrative of biblical studies, we find that these two elements govern the way method is done. In understanding the biblical text, exegesis is the primary method, with a focus either on the text itself (language, grammar, historical-cultural setting) or on identifying the nature of the text using a variety of critical methodologies (tradition, source, form, redaction, etc.) which leads then to a nuanced interpretation of the meaning or meanings. This is where the *Framework* element, Searching as Strategic Exploration, can have value in helping students to focus on identifying in their searches the varying approaches used by disciplinary researchers in their work.[28]

Question #2: What alternative methods
are gaining acceptance in biblical studies?
Students need to know that the method employed in any piece of biblical analysis is often the product of a particular biblical studies metanarrative variation. Is this a redaction study, a study employing source criticism, or a form critical study? Is the intent grammatical-historical study of the text at face value or is its goal to fracture colonial understandings of the text to understand it better in a post-colonial world? Search, within biblical studies writing, has to be strategic in order to draw out the emphases and beliefs behind them.

Our current search tools, unfortunately, do not provide filters to separate out the various methodologies (as does a database like PsycINFO). This means that students need to have eyes to see beyond the mere words in book and article titles to the metanarrative-driven methods that underlie these works.

Whether the methodological approach involves grammatical analysis, redaction history, or post-colonial criticism,[29] students need to pay attention to the presuppositions that govern method. In the face of such complexity, a student can use the categories of epistemology, metanarrative and method as roadmaps to move intelligently into each of these critical worlds.

Theological Studies as a Discipline

We have devoted considerable space to biblical studies in order to demonstrate that disciplines can be complex and that students being enculturated into a discipline need to understand multiple and various signposts. As our first discipline showed, there may well be a core knowledge base, mainstream metanarrative and agreed-upon methods, but there are also multiple variations.

Theological Studies: Epistemology

Question #1—What is the most essential knowledge in the discipline?
Of all the disciplines of theological education, theology represents the greatest diversity. On one hand, theology can be viewed as an expression of the convictions of the church (in each of its many forms and beliefs), thus making theological statements equivalent to faith statements. On the other, theology has long been an object of academic study. For seminarians, it is (and needs to be) both, since theological education is rigorous but has practice as its goal.

To delineate the essential knowledge base of theology, we need first to define the term "theology." A conservative approach would argue: "More precisely, the word [theology] denotes teaching about God and his relation to the world from creation to the consummation, particularly as it is set forth in an ordered, coherent manner."[30] Other scholars, operating outside of a conservative mindset, find it exceedingly difficult these days to define theology, now that this discipline has shattered into multiple approaches. Yet even these scholars will argue that there is a coherent epistemology. John Kent writes: "The final authority of Scripture and tradition remains unimpaired, however diverse interpretation may become: although there are many cases in which Scripture and tradition settle nothing, nothing can be settled apart from them."[31]

We thus find two foundations for theology's knowledge base: The Christian Scriptures and the tradition that has developed around them from their writing to the present day.

Question #2—How did the knowledge base develop over time?
The doing of theology is as old as the writing of the Christian Scriptures themselves in that later biblical writers often drew theological themes from earlier writers.

It is not difficult for theological students to discover the history (tradition) of theological thinking and to recognize the importance of the work of the Church Fathers, Scholastics, Reformers, Counter-Reformers, and so on, to the knowledge base of theology. While all of this developed through forces that the *Framework* would describe with the concepts, Authority is Constructed and Conceptual, and Scholarship as a Conversation, students need to see that the knowledge base of theology is a negotiated one. Innumerable writings over the history of the church were discounted or disputed to such an extent that they were ultimately deemed not authoritative. Others have risen to generally accepted status (Augustine,

Aquinas, Luther, and so on). Newer theologians all face evaluation by the disciplinary academy. Some of their works will survive the passage of time, while others will not.

Theological Studies: Metanarrative

Question #1—What motivates theologians?

It may seem simplistic to argue that theologians are devoted to understanding their world in the context of the Divine, but this is foundational. In this sense, theology is inquiry.[32] It is a quest to know and understand the Divine in relationship with the world, and thus to act. While it can have a purely academic motive, most often theologizing seeks to bear some fruit to improve human understanding, to probe difficult issues, or even to improve the human condition. Yet the motivation to do theology is tempered by the contexts within which theologians find themselves. Franke argues: "It is not the intent of theology simply to set forth, amplify, refine, and defend a timeless and fixed orthodoxy."[33] We must recognize that theologians are seekers and interpreters. Even if they believe in an infallible Scripture, all discussion that arises from it is the work of humans living in context. Just as authority is constructed and contextual,[34] so theologians recognize that their work is human and very much based both on their presuppositions and on the contexts in which they function.

The twentieth-century division between conservative (focusing on theology rooted in the biblical text and traditions congruent with it) and liberal (focusing on doing theology that is congruent with the modern world's understanding of itself and its aspirations) has now fragmented. The two main streams are actually based on a more foundational context, sometimes described as "theology from above" and "theology from below." Paul Tillich provided a good deal of clarity to the distinction by referring to "kerygmatic theology" and "apologetic, or answering, theology."[35] The former is theology from above practiced within the believing community. It is intended to inform the church of its belief system derived from Scripture and tradition. The latter is a theology that considers crucial questions in the larger world and attempts to respond to them theologically, thus starting from below in the world of humans.

Each theology has its risks. Kerygmatic approaches resist dialogue with other systems of thought and thus can be insular. Answering theology must not forget its roots. As Tillich argues regarding the latter: "It loses itself if it is not based on the kerygma as the substance and criterion of each of its statements."[36] Most theologians today offer a blend of the two, giving them differing emphases.

Question #2—How diverse is the theological studies metanarrative?

The metanarrative of theology has, in the past century, become exceedingly diverse. This can be attributed to a variety of factors, though the growth of Postmodernism is seen as a key driver. Van Huyssteen argued: "Even the briefest overview of our contemporary theological landscape reveals the startling fragmentation caused by what is commonly called 'the postmodern challenge' of our times."[37]

This should not cause the theological student to despair, because there are common patterns through the diversity. One represents the distinction between theologies from above and below. Within kerygmatic approaches we find three major streams: biblical theology (focus on theology as woven through the biblical narrative), systematic theology, and historical theology. Most theologians devote themselves to one or another of those streams, though overlap and even integration of approaches are possible. For answering theologies, there is generally a distinct interest in a specific issue: post-colonialism, liberation, feminism, and so on.

A second pattern distinguishes between those who take philosophical approaches to theology (something that has existed since the Church Fathers) or a biblical and tradition-based orientation. Among the latter, many theologians decry the influence of non-Christian philosophies, from Platonism to Postmodernism, on theological work.

Theological Studies: Method

Question #1: What are the standard methods used in theological studies?

*Question #2: What alternative methods are
gaining acceptance in theological studies?*

For theology, method is driven by metanarrative and epistemology. The values you hold regarding the theological task determine the methods you will choose and the knowledge base you affirm. Each type of theology has its own method, with variants. Thus, for example, a biblical theologian generally has little concern to systematize his/her work outside of the embedded narrative, a historical theologian is most interested in the discussions of theology through history, and a liberation theologian enlists the Bible and theology to form a response to the oppressed and to the oppressive systems in the world.

The methods thus vary, and theological students must remain vitally aware of the context within which they are working, both its motivations and the knowledge base it affirms. We can never assume that there is only one way to do theology.

Pastoral Theology as a Discipline

We now turn to a discipline that is less text-based and more oriented toward practice. Within pastoral theology we include a variety of sub-topics: pastoral care, preaching, teaching, pastoral counseling, Christian education, and so on. Though there is a great deal of diversity, pastoral theology unites itself in praxis, that is, putting belief and theory into practice. As such, it is based in other disciplines like biblical studies, theology and church history rather than simply being a set of skills divorced from other theological subjects. At the same time, it is guided by newer disciplines such as sociology, psychology, justice studies, and so on. Browning, in the Theology and Pastoral Care series from Fortress Press, spells out the emphases and potential tensions in its series foreword: "Our purpose ... [is to] (1) retrieve the theological and ethical foundations of the Judeo-Christian tradition for pastoral care, (2) develop lines of communication between pastoral theology and other disciplines of theology, (3) create an ecumenical dialogue on pastoral care, and (4) do this in such a way as to affirm, yet go beyond, the recent preoccupation of pastoral care with secular psychotherapy and other social sciences."[38]

"Pastoral Theology" as a term is well chosen. The praxis of ministry is immersed in theological thinking. Pamela and Michael Cooper-White, for example, stress that, "Practices of ministry ... do not exist apart from theology."[39] Thus, whatever direction it takes, pastoral theology is not mere social work or secular counseling. It only achieves its purposes in the context of the biblical-theological foundation that defines it.

Pastoral Theology: Epistemology
Pastoral theology has a knowledge base, which in some ways is ancient and in others changes constantly with transformations in society.

Question #1—What is the most essential knowledge in the discipline?
Like theology itself, pastoral theology can be a discipline from above or from below, though many pastoral theologians practice elements of both. From above, the knowledge base of theology rests in biblical teaching and the various traditions of ministry practice that have come down to us through the centuries. Pastoral theologians from above stress that the Bible itself is the primary source for true ministry praxis, and that this source has been further enhanced by the

traditions that interpreted biblical instruction about pastoral work. Secondary literature in this mode of thinking seeks to interpret biblical and theological mandates in terms of praxis.

Alternatively, many pastoral theologians today are not content simply to be informed by the Bible and tradition, as if their theology dictates their practice in every way. For them, the traditional knowledge base has its value but so does new thinking in which praxis informs a reinterpretation of theology or even develops new theological thinking. Cooper and Cooper argue: "Practical theologians … are generally no longer content merely to apply received dogma, but as of the later twentieth-century claimed the authority of practices themselves to instruct and inform theological reflection."[40] Thus new publications in the field can move beyond tradition to forge new thinking and updated theological understanding.

Question #2—How did the knowledge base develop over time?

The knowledge in pastoral theology is a result of a long history of reflection on practice. Over time, pastoral theologians have recounted their experiences, published guides and theoretical pieces, and gradually shaped our thinking about ministry as theological praxis. Newer voices are involved in rethinking old ideas or shaping new ones. Since this discipline's writings emerge out of reflection and instruction based in experience, the newer voices tend to be practitioners as often as they are scholars with high-level academic credentials. Thus, students of pastoral theology may well find that the authors they respect lack doctorates but have years or decades of experience.

Pastoral Theology: Metanarrative

As with most disciplines of theological education today, the metanarrative of pastoral theology is fragmenting. While there is a foundational cultural understanding among pastoral theologians, there are also variants that can put the culture at odds with itself.

Question #1—What motivates pastoral theologians?

Pastoral theologians function as mediators between belief and action. As Steyn and Masango have argued, "Not only should practical theology be energised by its theology, it should also, as its name implies, be practical in its nature, offering help to all people in need of pastoral care."[41] With regard to the latter, where theology is interpreted to provide such help, the work of pastoral theology is cultural and methodological, enlisting whatever tools are available to determine both needs and responses. Browning probably said it best when he argued:

For a practical theology to be genuinely practical, it must have some description of the present situation, some critical theory about the ideal situation, and some understanding of the processes, spiritual forces, and technologies required to get from where we are to the future ideal, no matter how fragmentarily and incompletely that ideal can be realized.[42]

Question #2—How diverse is the pastoral theology metanarrative?

Because pastoral theology involves praxis, its metanarrative can serve many different goals as various pastoral theologians deal with different needs.

Some, for example, have a problem with the individualism of much of pastoral theology, arguing that pastoral theologians must also be concerned with the larger community.[43] Others find their ethos in social justice, arguing that we cannot properly help people until societal structures and abuses are overcome. For them, the metanarrative echoes that of famous Christian activists like Martin Luther King.

Since pastoral theology covers a wide range of types of ministries, metanarratives may be expressed in a passion for preaching, religious education, pastoral counseling, and so on. Each shapes the common metanarrative of praxis with its own interests and emphases.

Pastoral Theology: Method

Question #1: What are the standard methods used in pastoral theology?

Question #2: What alternative methods are gaining acceptance in pastoral theology?

When it comes to method, the things pastoral theologians do are too numerous to describe here. We have a clear link between epistemology (especially secondary literature) and method in that the major methodological advances are made by practitioners who write about their work, their methods, and their goals. From there, the scholarly conversation is at work as pastoral theologians critique and build upon one another's work. The literature is expansive, and new methods are constantly being initiated. Jaison writes of pastoral theology: "It is a critical, constructive and grounded theological reflection by communities of faith, carried on consistently in the contexts of their 'praxis', which here denotes a combination of knowledge born of analytical objectivity and distance, practical wisdom and creative skills."[44]

Pastoral theologians enlist many of the other disciplines of working with people–psychotherapy, sociology, public speaking, education–but they "sanctify" those methods by putting them into the context of theologically interpreted praxis.

Finding a Path to Disciplinary Inclusion

We have considered a method of disciplinary analysis that leads to a deeper understanding of how three sample theological education disciplines function. The same could be done with the other disciplines. We have seen that the *Framework,* particularly the concepts Authority is Constructed and Contextual, Research as Inquiry, Scholarship as a Conversation, and Searching as Strategic Exploration, provide understandings that can help such disciplinary analysis.

Two questions emerge. First, how can understanding of disciplines through the model described above actually help students to enter into disciplines so that their articulation and research are done at a level of insiders rather than outsiders? Second, what role can librarians take in the task of helping theological students become disciplinarians? Let us address each question in turn.

Disciplinary Understanding and Enculturation

Our students come to us as relative outsiders to the disciplines they will be studying. They may have some undergraduate religious or theological education, but not at the level that will help them properly belong. Their professors are passionate about their subjects, prone to jargon and concepts that sometimes go over their students' heads (as many librarians can attest to having heard from students). For students, starting in a course is like entering a conversation at mid-point, knowing that the discussion has a history but failing to grasp what that history might entail.

When it comes to research and writing, students often lack understanding of the nature of the knowledge base, the way authors in a discipline comport themselves and engage in the scholarly conversation, and the common methods and conventions of expression favored by the discipline.

Disciplinary analysis around the themes of epistemology, metanarrative, and method, can open up a discipline to the kind of understanding that goes deeper than knowing content, and instead moves into the very culture of those who practice it. While experience in the discipline is required to deepen the enculturation, disciplinary analysis can form an entry point to making that deeper cultural understanding happen.

The Role of Librarians

Many theological librarians have few venues to enable disciplinary analysis. Why, then, are we even considering using such a model in our work? We do this for one simple reason: Librarians are well equipped to think in terms of disciplinary cultures while faculty, as diligent as they are, can struggle to find time and means to impart enculturation to their students, simply hoping it will happen to some measure.

This is a unique opportunity for librarians to bring the value of their work into the academy by engaging with faculty regarding the following:

1. Our students struggle with research. They often do not understand our assignments and write in ways unfamiliar to our disciplines.
2. Imparting knowledge and showing students how to use databases for research is not enough to make them disciplinary practitioners. We see evidence of that in the often low quality of their written work.
3. The problem is that students have not yet been enculturated into our disciplines.
4. As academic librarians, we have a model that may help.

So how would you as a librarian use this model? You could simply introduce it to faculty. You could co-teach a session with a faculty member in a student classroom in which you would explain elements of the model, and the professor would articulate the content of the discipline's epistemology, metanarrative and method. You and the professor could co-develop guides to the cultures of the professor's discipline, offering links to representative writing or statements of preferred method. Your reference interviews with students could include elements of disciplinary analysis that explain how to best research and write a project.

You can work with faculty to develop learning outcomes and assignment templates built around perceived gaps in student knowledge and skills related to functioning within a discipline. This would involve having faculty articulate the goals they want students to reach and then designing assignments to meet those goals.[45]

It is important for us to help students become insiders. The theological librarian has a vital place in that work. For more guidance on practical ways to implement disciplinary analysis in our work as librarians interacting with faculty, see *https://libguides.twu.ca/DisciplinaryEnculturation*.

Bibliography

Association of College and Research Libraries. *Framework for Information Literacy in Higher Education*. Chicago: American Library Association, 2016.

Becher, Tony. "The Significance of Disciplinary Differences." *Studies in Higher Education* 19, no. 2 (June 1994): 151. doi:10.1080/03075079412331382007.

Becher, Tony and Paul R. Trowler. *Academic Tribes and Territories: Intellectual Enquiry and the Cultures of Disciplines*. 2nd ed. Philadephia: The Society for Research into Higher Education & Open University, 2001.

Billett, Stephen. "Situated Learning: Bridging Sociocultural and Cognitive Theorising." *Learning and Instruction* 6, no. 3 (1996): 263–80.

Brown, John Seely and Paul Duguid. "Organizational Learning and Communities of Practice: Toward a Unified View of Working, Learning, and Innovation." *Organization Science* 2, no. 1 (1991): 40–57.

Browning, Don S. "Practical Theology and Political Theology." *Theology Today* 42, no. 1 (April 1985): 15–33.

———. "Series Foreword." In *Pastoral Care and Hermeneutics*, edited by Donald Capps. Theology and Pastoral Care, 9–10. Philadelphia: Fortress Press, 1984.

Budiselić, Ervin. "An Apology of Theological Education: The Nature, the Role, the Purpose, the Past and the Future of Theological Education." *Kairos: Evangelical Journal of Theology* 7, no. 2 (July 2013): 131–54.

Carter, Stacy M. and Miles Little. "Justifying Knowledge, Justifying Method, Taking Action: Epistemologies, Methodologies, and Methods in Qualitative Research." *Qualitative Health Research* 17, no. 10 (December 2007): 1316–28.

Cooper-White, Pamela and Michael L. Cooper-White. *Exploring Practices of Ministry*. Minneapolis: Fortress Press, 2014.

Edgar, Brian. "The Theology of Theological Education." *Evangelical Review of Theology* 29, no. 3 (2005): 208–17.

Farrell, Robert and William Badke. "Situating Information Literacy in the Disciplines: A Practical and Systematic Approach for Academic Librarians." *Reference Services Review* 43, no. 2 (2015): 319–40.

Fee, Gordon D. *New Testament Exegesis: A Handbook for Students and Pastors*. Louisville, KY: Westminster John Knox Press, 2002.

Finnin, William M. "The Sociality of Love as Theological Foundation for Pastoral Care and Counseling." *Iliff Review* 37, no. 3 (Fall 1980): 39–51.

Fordham, Michael. "Teachers and the Academic Disciplines." *Journal of Philosophy of Education* 50, no. 3 (August 2016): 419–31. doi:10.1111/1467-9752.12145.

Franke, John R. *The Character of Theology: An Introduction to Its Nature, Task, and Purpose*. Grand Rapids: Baker Academic, 2005.

Graham, Elspeth, and Joe Doherty. "Postmodern Horizons." In *Postmodernism and the Social Sciences*, edited by Elspeth Graham, Joe Doherty, and Mo Malek, 196–220. London: Palgrave Macmillan, 1992.

Hagen, Kenneth George. "Does Method Drive Biblical Study?" *Logia* 10, no. 1 (Epiphany 2001): 37–40.

Hauser, Alan J. and Duane Frederick Watson. *A History of Biblical Interpretation*. Grand Rapids: Eerdmans, 2003–2009.

Hayes, John Haralson and Carl R. Holladay. *Biblical Exegesis: A Beginner's Handbook*. Louisville, KY: Westminster John Knox Press, 2007.

Jaison, Jessy. "Practical Theology: A Transformative Praxis in Theological Education Towards Holistic Formation." *Journal of Theological Education and Mission* (2010): 1–13. Retrieved from *https://pdfs.semanticscholar.org/da3f /15282691848af2a8477a2c2c205a74403aca.pdf*.

Kent, John. "The Character and Possibility of Christian Theology Today." In *Companion Encyclopedia of Theology*, edited by Peter Byrne and J. L. Houlden, 875–94. London: Routledge, 1995.

Lambek, Michael. "Recognizing Religion: Disciplinary Traditions, Epistemology, and History." *Numen: International Review for the History of Religions* 61, no. 2/3 (April 2014): 145–65. doi:10.1163/15685276-12341313.

Lave, Jean and Etienne Wenger. *Situated Learning: Legitimate Peripheral Participation*. Cambridge: Cambridge University Press, 1991.

Lieu, Judith and J. W. Rogerson, eds. *The Oxford Handbook of Biblical Studies*. Oxford: OUP Oxford, 2006.

Lipponen, Lasse. "Information Literacy as Situated and Distributed Activity." In *Practising Information Literacy: Bringing Theories of Learning, Practice and Information Literacy Together*, edited by A. Annemaree Lloyd and Sanna Talja, 51–64. Wagga, NSW: Wagga Centre for Information Studies, Charles Stuart University, 2010.

Masango, Maake J. and Tobias H. Steyn. "The Theology and Praxis of Practical Theology in the Context of the Faculty of Theology." *HTS Teologiese Studies/Theological Studies* 67, no. 2 (2011): e1-e7. doi:10.4102/hts.v67i2.956.

Merton, Robert K. "The Normative Structure of Science" (1942). In Merton, Robert K. *The Sociology of Science*, edited by Norman W. Storer, 265–78. Chicago: University of Chicago Press, 1973.

Nichols, James T. "The 3 Directions: Situated Information Literacy." *College & Research Libraries* 70, no. 6 (2009): 515–30.

Pedynowski, Dena. "Science(s): Which, When and Whose? Probing the Metanarrative of Scientific Knowledge in the Social Construction of Nature." *Progress in Human Geography* 27, no. 6 (2003): 735–52.

Reventlow, Henning Graf. *History of Biblical Interpretation*. Atlanta: Society of Biblical Literature, 2009-2010.

Scholz, Susanne, ed. *Biblical Studies Alternatively: An Introductory Reader.* Upper Saddle River, NJ: Prentice Hall, 2003.

Segovia, Fernando F. *Decolonizing Biblical Studies: A View from the Margins.* Maryknoll, NY: Orbis Books, 2000.

Shepherd, Massey H. "What Should a Commentary Be or Do?" In *The Commentary Hermeneutically Considered,* edited by Edward C. Hobbs, 1-4. Berkeley, CA: Center for Hermeneutical Studies and Modern Culture, 1978.

Simmons, Michelle Holschuh. "Librarians as Disciplinary Discourse Mediators: Using Genre Theory to Move Toward Critical Information Literacy." *portal: Libraries and the Academy* 5, no. 3 (2005): 297-311.

Smith, Kevin G. "Integrated Theology: A Key to Training Thinking Practitioners." *Conspectus (South African Theological Seminary)* 12 (September 2011): 185-98.

Tillich, Paul. *Systematic Theology.* Chicago: University of Chicago Press, 1967.

Van Huyssteen, J. Wentzel. "Tradition and the Task of Theology." *Theology Today* 55, no. 2 (1998): 213-28.

Wang, Li. "An Information Literacy Integration Model and its Application in Higher Education." *Reference Services Review* 39, no. 4 (2011): 703-20.

Wright. D. F. "Theology." In *New Dictionary of Theology,* edited by Martin Davie, Tim Grass, Stephen R. Holmes, John McDowell, and Thomas A. Noble, 903-4. Downers Grove: IVP Academic, 2016.

Notes

1. Brian Edgar, "The Theology of Theological Education," *Evangelical Review of Theology* 29, no. 3 (2005): 208–17; Kevin G. Smith, "Integrated Theology: A Key to Training Thinking Practitioners," *Conspectus (South African Theological Seminary)* 12 (September 2011): 185–98; Ervin Budiselić, "An Apology of Theological Education: The Nature, the Role, the Purpose, the Past and the Future of Theological Education," *Kairos: Evangelical Journal of Theology* 7, no. 2 (July 2013): 131–54.

2. Jean Lave and Etienne Wenger, *Situated Learning: Legitimate Peripheral Participation* (Cambridge: Cambridge University Press, 1991); Stephen Billett, "Situated Learning: Bridging Sociocultural and Cognitive Theorising," *Learning and instruction* 6, no. 3 (1996): 263–80.

3. Association of College and Research Libraries, *Framework for Information Literacy in Higher Education* (Chicago: American Library Association, 2016).

4. Michael Fordham has argued cogently that teaching is not a generic exercise but that teachers are disciplinary practitioners engaged in the discipline they teach. Michael Fordham, "Teachers and the Academic Disciplines," *Journal of Philosophy of Education* 50, no. 3 (August 2016): 419–31, doi:10.1111/1467-9752.12145.

5. Lave and Wenger, 27ff.

6. James T. Nichols, "The 3 Directions: Situated Information Literacy," *College & Research Libraries* 70, no. 6 (2009): 515–30; Lasse Lipponen, "Information Literacy as Situated and Distributed Activity," in *Practising Information Literacy: Bringing Theories of Learning, Practice and Information Literacy Together,* ed. Annemaree Lloyd and Sanna Talja (Wagga, NSW: Wagga Centre for Information Studies, Charles Stuart University, 2010): 51–64; Li Wang, "An Information Literacy Integration Model and its Application in Higher Education," *Reference Services Review* 39, no. 4 (2011): 703–20; Robert Farrell and William Badke, "Situating Information Literacy in the Disciplines: A Practical and Systematic Approach for Academic Librarians," *Reference Services Review* 43, no. 2 (2015): 319–40.

7. Lave and Wenger, 89ff.

8. Farrell and Badke, 323.

9. Compare Merton, who describes these three elements as "accumulated knowledge," "cultural values and mores," and "characteristic methods." He views the three as vitally interrelated. Robert K. Merton, "The Normative Structure of Science" (1942), in Robert K. Merton, *The Sociology of Science,* ed. Norman W. Storer (Chicago: University of Chicago Press, 1973), 265–78. Carter and Little use the terms "epistemology," "methodology," and "method," meaning in turn, "justification of knowledge," "justification for the methods of a research project," and "research action." Stacy M. Carter and Miles Little, "Justifying Knowledge, Justifying Method, Taking Action: Epistemologies, Methodologies, and Methods in Qualitative Research," *Qualitative Health Research* 17, no. 10 (December 2007): 1316–28.

10. ACRL, *Framework.*

11. Michael Lambek, "Recognizing Religion: Disciplinary Traditions, Epistemology, and History," *Numen: International Review for the History of Religions* 61, no. 2/3 (April 2014): 168, doi:10.1163/15685276-12341313.

12. Lave and Wenger, *Situated Learning,* 89ff. This concept was also described in John Seely Brown and Paul Duguid, "Organizational Learning and Communities of Practice: Toward a Unified View of Working, Learning, and Innovation," *Organization Science* 2, no. 1 (1991), 40–57.

13. Elspeth Graham, for example, argues that the deniers of metanarratives themselves operate within their own metanarrative: "Postmodernism rejects metanarratives like those which underpin modernism. Yet postmodernism ... also appears to rely upon metanarrative." Elspeth Graham and Joe Doherty, "Postmodern Horizons," in *Postmodernism and the Social Sciences,* ed. Elspeth Graham, Joe Doherty, and Mo Malek (London: Palgrave Macmillan, 1992), 208.

14. ACRL, *Framework.* For more on metanarratives in disciplines, and critiques of metanarrative theory, see: Tony Becher, "The Significance of Disciplinary Differences," *Studies in Higher Education* 19, no. 2 (June 1994): 151, doi:10.1080/03075079412331382007; Tony Becher and Paul R. Trowler, *Academic Tribes and Territories: Intellectual Enquiry and the Cultures of Disciplines,* 2nd ed. (Philadephia: The Society for Research into Higher Education & Open University, 2001); Dena Pedynowski, "Science(s): Which, When and Whose? Probing the Metanarrative of Scientific Knowledge in the Social Construction of Nature," *Progress in Human Geography* 27, no. 6 (2003): 735–52.

15. Carter and Little, for example, demonstrate how epistemology is made visible through method so that the two are intertwined, as illustrated in their framework for evaluating the quality of a particular method in the social sciences ("Justifying Method, Justifying Knowledge").

16. Michelle Holschuh Simmons, "Librarians as Disciplinary Discourse Mediators: Using Genre Theory to Move Toward Critical Information Literacy," *portal: Libraries and the Academy* 5, no. 3 (2005): 306.

17. Wenderoth, Christine. "Research Behaviors of Theological Educators and Students: The Known and Unknown," *American Theological Library Association Summary of Proceedings* 61 (2007): 178–83. Perhaps the most significant sign that faculty are not yet addressing this issue is the fact that there is almost no higher education literature on student research ability development except for that provided by librarians.

18. A small sampling would include Alan J. Hauser and Duane Frederick Watson, *A History of Biblical Interpretation* (Grand Rapids: Eerdmans, 2003–2009); Henning Graf Reventlow, *History of Biblical Interpretation* (Atlanta: Society of Biblical Literature, 2009-2010).

19. Kenneth George Hagen, "Does Method Drive Biblical Study?" *Logia* 10, no. 1 (Epiphany 2001): 39.

20. Hagen, 39.

21. For a sense of the variety of biblical scholarship over past decades see: "Part One: On the Discipline," in *The Oxford Handbook of Biblical Studies*, ed. Judith Lieu and J. W. Rogerson (Oxford: Oxford University Press, 2006), 1–132.

22. Massey H. Shepherd, "What Should a Commentary Be or Do?" in *The Commentary Hermeneutically Considered*, ed. Edward C. Hobbs (Berkeley, CA: Center for Hermeneutical Studies and Modern Culture, 1978), 1.

23. Some scholars decry a presuppositional approach, however. Hagen argues: "The task of interpretation is to lay out the message of Scripture. Otherwise it is ripped out of historical context and made to float on the horizons of Western philosophical inquiry" (p. 39).

24. Gordon D. Fee, *New Testament Exegesis: A Handbook for Students and Pastors* (Louisville, KY: Westminster John Knox, 2002), 1.

25. John Haralson Hayes and Carl R. Holladay, *Biblical Exegesis: A Beginner's Handbook* (Louisville, KY: Westminster John Knox Press, 2007), 16.

26. John Barton, ed., *The Cambridge Companion to Biblical Interpretation* (Cambridge: Cambridge University Press, 1998).

27. For further examples of diverse metanarratives in action, see Susanne Scholz, ed., *Biblical Studies Alternatively: An Introductory Reader* (Upper Saddle River, NJ: Prentice Hall, 2003).

28. ACRL, *Framework*.

29. This concept, which may seem somewhat obscure to students, is well described in Fernando F. Segovia, *Decolonizing Biblical Studies: A View from the Margins* (Maryknoll, NY: Orbis Books, 2000).

30. D. F. Wright, "Theology," in *New Dictionary of Theology*, ed. Martin Davie et al. (Downers Grove: IVP Academic, 2016), 904.

31. John Kent, "The Character and Possibility of Christian Theology Today," in *Companion Encyclopedia of Theology*, ed. Peter Byrne and J. L. Houlden (London: Routledge, 1995), 875.

32. Compare the ACRL *Framework* threshold concept, "Searching as Strategic Inquiry," along with its knowledge practices and dispositions.

33. John R. Franke, *The Character of Theology: An Introduction to Its Nature, Task, and Purpose* (Grand Rapids: Baker Academic, 2005), 84.

34. ACRL, *Framework*.

35. Paul Tillich, *Systematic Theology* (Chicago: University of Chicago Press, 1967), vol. 1, 6–8.

36. Tillich, vol. 1, 7.

37. J. Wentzel Van Huyssteen, "Tradition and the Task of Theology," *Theology Today* 55, no. 2 (1998): 213.

38. Don S. Browning, "Series Foreword," in *Pastoral Care and Hermeneutics,* ed. Donald Capps, Theology and Pastoral Care (Philadelphia: Fortress Press, 1984), 9.

39. Pamela Cooper-White and Michael L. Cooper-White, *Exploring Practices of Ministry* (Minneapolis: Fortress Press, 2014), 12.

40. Cooper-White and Cooper-White, 19.

41. Maake J. Masango and Tobias H. Steyn, "The Theology and Praxis of Practical Theology in the Context of the Faculty of Theology," *HTS Teologiese Studies/Theological Studies* 67, no. 2 (2011): e1-e7, doi:10.4102/hts.v67i2.956.

42. Don S. Browning, "Practical Theology and Political Theology," *Theology Today* 42, no. 1 (April 1985): 20.

43. William M. Finnin, "The Sociality of Love as Theological Foundation for Pastoral Care and Counseling," *Iliff Review* 37, no. 3 (Fall 1980): 39–51.

44. Jessy Jaison, "Practical Theology: A Transformative Praxis in Theological Education Towards Holistic Formation," *Journal of Theological Education and Mission* (2010): 1–13, retrieved from *https://pdfs.semanticscholar.org /da3f/15282691848af2a8477a2c2c205a74403aca.pdf*

45. See Farrell and Badke.

Praxis

CHAPTER 5

Charting Information Literacy

Curriculum Mapping at an Embedded Seminary

ELIZABETH YOUNG MILLER, MORAVIAN COLLEGE AND MORAVIAN THEOLOGICAL SEMINARY

L OCATED IN BETHLEHEM, PENNSYLVANIA, MORAVIAN THEOLOGICAL Seminary (MTS) offers several degrees and certificates. In addition to the Master of Divinity (MDiv), students can earn a Master of Arts in Theological Studies (MATS), Chaplaincy (MACh), and/or Clinical Counseling (MACC). Certificates are available in formative spirituality and spiritual direction. Currently the Seminary enrolls 46 full-time equivalents.[1]

Students and faculty alike benefit from the seminary's relationship with Moravian College, a private liberal arts college. College and seminary resources are pooled, and one library serves all students. Not only do I serve as the library's seminary liaison, but I also provide instruction, outreach, and reference services to undergraduate students. Therefore, I look for library practice applications useful across user populations.

Project Beginnings

In the spring of 2016, scholarship on curriculum mapping began to pique my interest. During Moravian Theological Seminary's two-day curriculum meeting in May, dubbed the "marathon meeting," I listened attentively as faculty focused on curriculum review and established gating assessments (core assignments that students must pass in order to successfully advance in a degree program) for each program. I contemplated how these measures might fit with information literacy.[2] Keeping these thoughts in the back of my mind, the topic of curriculum mapping resonated with me at the American Theological Library Association (ATLA) Conference in June 2016. Desirae Zingarelli-Sweet's poster presentation

"Prepare a Way through the Wilderness: Transforming Library Instruction by Mapping the Curriculum"[3] inspired me to develop a plan for my institution. The next month, I met with the dean of the seminary to share conference highlights and pitched the idea of mapping the ACRL's *Framework* to the seminary's curriculum. The dean recommended beginning with the MATS program, and the Seminary's registrar promptly granted me access to course syllabi.[4] By the end of the summer, I was well underway with the curriculum mapping process.

Theory and Praxis

Due to changes in the landscape of higher education, librarians may feel an increasing need to assert their value. Higher education institutions grapple with a myriad of issues: economic pressures, declining enrollment, advances in technology, the public perception of the value of higher education, and more.[5] As a result, assessment, accountability, and information literacy become even more important, with librarians demonstrating their worth by showing how they contribute to the mission and goals of the institution and aid with retention and student success.[6] Curriculum mapping is one way librarians can showcase their value. As Timothy Lincoln at Austin Presbyterian Theological Seminary Library has argued, the curriculum and library use are closely intertwined, and he raises a relevant question: how does the library show that it supports the seminary's curriculum?[7] Curriculum mapping can serve as one answer. The purpose of curriculum mapping involves ensuring that goals tie to the work being done.[8]

In surveying the literature, most curriculum mapping occurs at the undergraduate level. Nonetheless, this scholarship holds meaning for seminaries and continues to encompass more disciplines.

While there is consensus that curriculum mapping is systematic, definitions vary and librarians and educators view curriculum mapping from different perspectives.[9] Librarians at Loyola Marymount University describe curriculum mapping as "a way of examining a program of study and the courses within the program in order to understand curriculum structures and relationships, gain insight in how students experience their discipline, and increase curricular content."[10] Medical educator R. M. Harden offers an even more robust definition: "Curriculum mapping is concerned with what is taught (the content, the areas of expertise addressed, and the learning outcomes), how it is taught (the learning resources, the learning opportunities), when it is taught (the timetable, the curriculum sequence), and the measures used to determine whether the student has achieved the expected learning outcomes (assessment)."[11] The links that curriculum mapping highlight are invaluable. Curriculum mapping identifies not only library instruction opportunities, but points out redundancies too.[12] Moreover, curriculum mapping provides a visual for scaffolding.[13] Curriculum mapping can show how library instruction supports course outcomes and assignments.[14]

Often, curriculum mapping focuses on learning outcomes. Megan Oakleaf defines learning outcomes as "what librarians hope students will be able to do as a result of instruction."[15] She emphasizes that learning outcomes require observable and measurable behaviors and, therefore, when formulated, active verbs should be chosen.[16] Ideally, the goals and objectives of the information literacy program should be in alignment with those of the library and institution as a whole. If so, library learning outcomes can be mapped to accreditation, departmental outcomes, and/or institutional learning outcomes.[17] Librarians at Cornell University took a slightly different approach, mapping library instruction to the institution's curriculum, but without including learning outcomes.[18]

Libraries have used curriculum mapping to focus on different contexts and content. In one case study, librarians targeted courses in, among other disciplines, religious studies, and mapped these to library learning outcomes.[19] More recently, librarians at Concordia College mapped the frames to required PEAK (Pivotal Experience in Applied Knowledge) projects, which are immersive capstones for graduating students.[20] At Pitts Community College, librarians mapped the general education curriculum to the older ACRL information literacy standards, [21] while at the University of Tennessee, librarians mapped science courses to those standards.[22] Many times, librarians will begin curriculum mapping by starting with courses required for a particular major.[23]

Before curriculum mapping became a buzzword, Douglas Gragg at Candler School of Theology advocated embedding information literacy into required courses.[24] Gragg's recommendation would work especially well if stand-alone concepts could be taught in required classes, for scaffolding information literacy concepts can be challenging especially with the absence of sequenced courses.[25] At Moravian Theological Seminary this is the case–students have required courses for each degree program but they are not always taken in a particular order. Focusing curriculum mapping on learning outcomes for a degree program then becomes wise and is a practice that some libraries adopt.[26] At Moravian, I began by mapping MATS gatekeeping measures to the ACRL frames and added learning outcomes for required courses. Some librarians include electives for each major in their curriculum mapping as well.[27] Librarians at Loyola Marymount University explain their process in detail; they record "the learning outcomes (what students do); the assignment (how the student demonstrates learning); the curriculum (what does the student need to know to do it well?); and how it is assessed or graded (how we know the student has done it well)."[28]

In addition to the curriculum itself, assessment is another key component of the curriculum mapping process. Extolling the importance of assessment, Syracuse University library science professor Megan Oakleaf emphasizes that assessment plans serve as tools to demonstrate "the value that academic librarians contribute to the teaching and learning mission of their institutions."[29] Curriculum mapping can serve as an assessment vehicle, and Standard 4 of the Association of Theological Schools (ATS) speaks directly to the role of the library. Standard 4.2 addresses the library's contributions to "learning, teaching, and research," and Standard 4.3 focuses on the library as a partner in curriculum development.[30] Oakleaf encourages librarians to become partners in the curriculum by discussing discipline-specific threshold concepts with teaching faculty to see how they overlap with information literacy and critical thinking skills.[31] William Badke, Associate Librarian for Associated Canadian Theological Schools and Information Literacy at Trinity Western University echoes Oakleaf's recommendation, urging librarians to collaborate with theology faculty members to create meaningful learning outcomes and corresponding assignments, supported by library instruction.[32]

Timothy Lincoln also provides insight for theological contexts. In examining the curriculum at Austin Presbyterian Theological Seminary, Lincoln focuses on curricular information demand (CID). He defines CID as "how a school's curriculum requires students to find, discover, and use information resources for non-field work courses."[33] He uses a table to map the intensity of a task to information-seeking behavior and, while not stated explicitly, information literacy concepts are present.[34] Lincoln then specifically targets classes with a moderate to high intensity level, many of which were MATS courses.[35] He also developed the acronym FRAU (find, retrieve, analyze and use), which he maps to courses in another table;[36] these mappings could be useful for a tiered approach to library instruction. His project could also easily be expanded by incorporating the new information literacy frames. Lincoln demonstrates that syllabi can be effective tools for measuring CID.[37] At Moravian, course syllabi served as a core resource for curriculum mapping.

Studying syllabi is not a new concept. In 1985, Jeremy Sayles highlighted that studying syllabi could improve library instruction.[38] Today, librarians can analyze syllabi to identify information literacy;[39] highlighting courses with a research component is an important step in the curriculum mapping process.[40] Starting with syllabi can be a good start, but examining the curriculum involves conversations with faculty, too. For Lincoln, CID was a great way to begin discussions with faculty about assignment collaboration.[41] My experience at Moravian was similar: sharing the curriculum mapping with faculty members helped with designing information literacy assessments.

Techniques

When it comes to curriculum mapping, there is no "one size fits all" technique. Nonetheless, certain methods may be more effective. If multiple librarians plan to contribute, using Google Sheets or a similar shared document can be useful.[42] Since I was the only librarian initially working on curriculum mapping at Moravian, I instead used an Excel spreadsheet. Incorporating symbols to designate the presence or absence of information literacy can also be beneficial.[43] For example, I used the color yellow to represent the presence of an information literacy session. Another library used a special background color to flag courses that required research but lacked library instruction in the last five years.[44]

Curriculum Mapping and the ACRL Frames

The first tab in Moravian's Excel spreadsheet charts how the gatekeeping measures (core assignments) identified by the seminary faculty align with the frames (Image 1). After completing this task, I solicited input from the information literacy coordinator to ensure that I was on the right track. Once she endorsed my work, I mapped course objectives for all required courses in the MATS degree to the frames.[45] Moravian teaching faculty developed both the course learning objectives and the gatekeeping measures.

Each required course has a separate Excel tab in the spreadsheet, and for each class I did my best to develop information literacy objectives. In Moravian's curriculum mapping spreadsheet, the information literacy frames are across the top of the document. Along the left side are course learning objectives, each one on a separate line;[46] please see Image 2 below for an example. In the curriculum mapping process, I also identified assignments and/or assessments that represent each of the ACRL frames.[47] Given the overlap among the frames, some assignments fall into more than one category.

IMAGE 1 - MATS Curriculum Mapping Spreadsheet

Authority is Constructed and Contextual	Information Creation as a Process	Information has Value	Research as Inquiry	Scholarship as Conversation	Searching as Strategic Exploration
Analyze primary research materials, demonstrating knowledge of larger contexts and ability to interpret scripture Gating Assessment: SEBK Texts in Context Paper	Analyze primary research materials, demonstrating knowledge of larger contexts and ability to interpret scripture Gating Assessment: SEBK 620 Interpretation Paper				
		Identify and engage diverse and overlapping cultural and social dynamics Gating Assessment: LinC? Portfolio?			
				Integrate social, historical, intellectual, and/or theological contexts of an object of study Gating Assessment: SETH 610 Final Assignment OR SECC 620 Final Assignment; SETH 630 Final Assignment	
		Independently identify, pursue, and acquire knowledge in the field of study Gating Assessment: SEIP 950: Initial annotated bibliography; Research tutorial with Seminary Liaison Librarian	Independently identify, pursue, and acquire knowledge in the field of study Gating Assessment: SEIP 950: Initial annotated bibliography; Research tutorial with Seminary Liaison Librarian	Independently identify, pursue, and acquire knowledge in the field of study Gating Assessment: SEIP 950: Initial annotated bibliography; Research tutorial with Seminary Liaison Librarian
			Identify a research issue, use primary research materials and discuss the issue in a coherent, thoroughly researched, integrative paper or project Gating Assessment: Thesis	Identify a research issue, use primary research materials and discuss the issue in a coherent, thoroughly researched, integrative paper or project Gating Assessment: Thesis	Identify a research issue, use primary research materials and discuss the issue in a coherent, thoroughly researched, integrative paper or project Gating Assessment: Thesis

Framework & Program Outcomes | SEBK 610 - Hebrew Bible | SEBK 620 - New Testament | SECC 601 - LinC | SECC 660 - World Religions | SEFS 601 - ... ⊕

IMAGE 1 - MATS Curriculum Mapping Spreadsheet

Information Literacy in Place as of Spring 2017	Authority is Constructed and Contextual	Information Creation as a Process	Information has Value	Research as Inquiry	Scholarship as Conversation	Searching as Strategic Exploration
Gain broad familiarity with the contents of the NT and other early Christian literature				Students will be able to use concordances and BibleWorks to aid in their interpretation of scripture		
Set the social world of nascent Christianity within a first-century context	Students will be able to analyze and incorporate various viewpoints in their Interpretation Paper (Gating Assessment)					
Learn and begin to gain facility with various modern methods for interpreting and theologically reflecting upon NT texts					Students will be able to synthesize and integrate secondary sources (articles, books, commentaries, etc.) into their Interpretation Paper (Gating Assessment)	
Explore the issue of the authority of scripture and the role of the Bible among various communities	Students will be able to explain how an author's background/worldview influences his/her interpretation of scripture					
Practice scholarly research, analytical argumentation, oral expression, the use of technology in academic expression, and academic writing		Students will be able to identify characteristics of scholarly articles as evidenced in the bibliography of their Interpretation Paper (Gating Assessment)	Students will be able to use Turabian/Chicago citation style to direct readers to their sources	Students will be able to develop a thesis statement that directs their research		

IMAGE 2 - *Introduction to New Testament* Curriculum Mapping

Authority is Constructed and Contextual

Key tenets of the frame Authority is Constructed and Contextual include context and perspective.[48] Cultural differences in geographic locations impact the interpretation of Scripture. This is certainly the case in the Global South, where culture factors into the understanding of the Bible.[49] According to the *Framework*, learning occurs when an audience is open to new perspectives.[50] Faculty at Moravian value this type of learning, recognizing, acknowledging, and celebrating multiple voices. As a result, several assignments map to the frame Authority is Constructed and Contextual, including the Texts in Context (TiC) paper for Hebrew Bible, the interpretation paper in New Testament, and the final paper in Christian Ethics.

Faculty at Moravian designated both the TiC paper and the interpretation paper as gating assessments for the MATS degree. The TiC paper requires students to "analyze primary research materials, demonstrate knowledge of larger contexts, and [be able] to interpret scripture."[51] William Badke provides a similar example that can be used in a biblical studies course: students can trace the research on a particular topic over time by examining the different perspectives scholars offer.[52] In terms of a learning objective for this type of assignment, for *Introduction to New Testament* I wrote that "students will be able to analyze and incorporate various viewpoints."[53] Certainly the frame Authority is Constructed and Contextual can be assessed by analyzing the sources students choose for their papers. Megan Oakleaf shares that students can demonstrate mastery of this frame "by brainstorm[ing] characteristics of authors deemed as trustworthy on a topic."[54] At Concordia College, librarians mapped Authority is Constructed and Contextual to first-year library instruction, focusing on the peer-review process.[55] While faculty certainly want students to use scholarly sources, the professor of New Testament and I wanted to move beyond merely checking for credible sources. Therefore, we collaborated on a rubric to assess the number, caliber, and diversity of sources (Table 1).[56] The rubric we developed can also assess Information Creation as a Process.[57]

	1	2	3	4
Number of sources Scholarship as Conversation	Paper contains less than 3 cited sources.	Paper contains between 3 and 5 cited sources.	Paper contains between 6 and 8 cited sources.	Paper contains more than 8 cited sources.
Caliber of resources Information Creation as a process Scholarship as a conversation	Primarily cites sources that fall into the category of popular literature.	Cites articles from popular literature, general interest publications, and trade/ professional serials. Primarily sites book that are more than 10 years old.	Cites articles from both trade/ professional publications and scholarly, peer-reviewed journals. Cites books from well-known commentary series and reputable publishers.	Orinearly cites scholarly, peer-reviewed articles and book from well-known commentary series and reputable publishers.
Diversity of sources Authority is Constructed and Contextual Scholarship as Conversation	Paper lack diversity, with sources either coming from the same author, publisher, and/or journal.	Paper shows some diversity with sources coming from 2 to 3 authors, publishers, and/or journals. Cited commentaries are broad and focus more than 1 book of the Bible.	Paper shows diversity with sources coming from 3 more authors, publishers, and/or journals. Cited commentaries focus on a single book of the Bible.	Paper shows diversity with sourcves coming from 4 or more authors, publishers, and/or journals. Cited commentaries focus on a single book of the Bible.

TABLE 1 - MTS *Introduction to New Testament* Bibliographic Analysis Rubric

Information Creation as a Process

The rubric category "caliber of resources" easily maps to the frame of Information Creation as a Process (see Table 1).[58] Information Creation as a Process values the peer review process.[59] Many faculty members want students to cite scholarly sources, including the New Testament professor with whom I was working. Not only was he looking for peer-reviewed articles, but he wanted students to incorporate recent scholarship too. Alas, with the departure of this professor, I have not had an opportunity to assess student bibliographies for *Introduction to New Testament*. However, I may be able to use this rubric with student bibliographies from Hebrew Bible.[60]

Badke offers another way to approach this frame, utilizing primary and secondary sources. He explains that students in a church history course could identify a primary document and show how this material influences secondary sources and, in the process, identify key secondary literature on a topic.[61]

Information Has Value

Information Has Value emphasizes the importance of intellectual property and proper attribution.[62] The library instruction I offer to students in the course *Learning in Community* (LinC) highlights the importance of academic integrity, and since all seminary students, regardless of program, must complete this course, the content reaches the entire seminary student population. In LinC, I present students with a series of scenarios asking them to first decide if the situations are examples of plagiarism and then prompting them to explain their rationale.[63] Currently, LinC is under review, and it appears that, moving forward, I will be fully integrated into this course, meeting with students in each degree program during their first semester to discuss discipline specific resources in addition to plagiarism. As a result, I hope to design assessments to measure not only this frame but others as well.

Librarians at other institutions have also focused on this frame. For example, the work of librarians Rebecca Kuglitsch and Peggy Burge maps to Information Has Value. Kuglitsch and Burge begin their citation management sessions by asking students to reflect on and name their frustrations with citations.[64] They view these workshops as an ideal intermediate step appropriate for sophomores. By the time students are working on a capstone project, it is too late and, given all the concepts covered during the first year, it is simply not feasible to cover this material earlier.[65] Timing these workshops, however, can be tricky. At Moravian, when I offered joint Zotero workshops for undergraduate and seminary students, few people attended, mirroring the experience of Kuglitsch and Burge. The solution for Kuglitsch and Burge involved offering library classes on demand; a group of classmates and/or friends could request a personalized citation workshop.[66] At Moravian, this idea seems worth trying with both seminary students and undergraduate honors students–two of the previous target audiences. Citation workshops fit nicely with academic integrity, something that faculty care deeply about, perhaps easing the buy-in process and reaching more departments.[67]

Research as Inquiry

Most programs of study relate in some form to the frame Research as Inquiry. The *Framework* notes that "[r]esearch is iterative and depends on asking increasingly complex or new questions whose answers in turn develop additional questions or lines of inquiry in any field."[68] Oakleaf notes that a measure of Research as Inquiry includes the ability "to list areas of consensus and disagreement among publications on a topic."[69] Critical essays, research proposals and papers, capstone projects, and theses map to this frame. With regard to the MATS program at Moravian, the research proposal for Hebrew Bible and the thesis align well with the frame Research as Inquiry. While I have not developed assessments that tie to this frame yet, the professor of Hebrew Bible values information literacy skills and has invited me to meet with her classes in the past.[70] She is now teaching the thesis prep course as well. Since the library receives copies of each student thesis, it will be relatively easy to evaluate them once an assessment measure is developed. The thesis required of all MATS students serves as the culminating gatekeeping measure for the degree and maps to multiple frames.

Scholarship as Conversation

Much overlap exists between Research as Inquiry and Scholarship as Conversation, and certainly this is the case with regard to the MATS thesis at Moravian. The frame Scholarship as Conversation invites students to add their voices to the scholarly conversation on a topic.[71] Four gating assessments at Moravian Theological Seminary align with this frame: the thesis, the annotated bibliography for the thesis prep course, the final paper in Christian ethics, and the interpretation paper for New Testament. According to the faculty learning objective for the thesis, students must "[i]dentify a research issue, use primary research materials and discuss the issue in a coherent, thoroughly researched, integrative paper or project."[72] I also mapped the course *Christian Theology* to the frame of Scholarship as Conversation, "hoping that students can contribute to the conversation surrounding the theologians they study."[73] The New Testament interpretation paper not only requires that students also use a variety of sources, but that they demonstrate synthesis and integration of these articles, books, commentaries, etc. All three categories on the bibliography rubric attempt to assess these skills (see Table 1), and I am currently creating an assessment for this final paper.[74]

Searching as Strategic Exploration

The frame Searching as Strategic Exploration may be the easiest frame to assess, for it focuses on brainstorming and search strategies. The *Framework* explains that "[s]earching for information is often nonlinear and iterative, requiring the evaluation of a range of information sources and the mental flexibility to pursue alternate avenues as new understanding develops."[75] To address this frame, I initially developed exercises and assessments for use with *Introduction to New Testament* and the thesis prep course. Over the last year, library colleagues and I have begun mapping the frame Searching as Strategic Exploration to undergraduate courses.

Introduction to New Testament

Teaching library instruction sessions for undergraduates influenced the search strategies form I created for use with students in *Intro to New Testament*. The exercise I developed helps students "get their feet wet" with the research process. During the spring 2018 library session for *Intro to New Testament*, I distributed this exercise (please see Table 2), which students completed before leaving the library.

Search Tool (e.g., online library catalog, database— specify name, Google)	Keyword(s) Used	# of Results	Modifications to Search (e.g., limiting by year, using synonyms and/or subject terms)	Citations

TABLE 2 - Search Strategies Form

To assess these worksheets, I created a search strategy checklist, focusing primarily on where students are searching and the modifications they are making.[76] The checklist directly assesses concepts covered during the library session. All eight students searched a database with students making anywhere from one to five search modifications; Table 3 provides a breakdown of these modifications.[77]

Search Modification	Number of Stuents Who Chose Option
Date	6
Full text	3
Language	3
Scripture/Bible citation search feature	1
Source type (e.g., scholarly peer-reviewed)	6
Subject terms	2

TABLE 3 - Search Strategy Assessment

As students progress through the MATS degree, their search skills should improve. Therefore, my initial goal was to utilize both the search checklist and the research log exercise to compare the progression of information literacy.[78] However, this data collection and analysis has not occurred yet.

Research Log

The thesis reflects the search prowess of MATS students. One of the course objectives listed in the syllabus for the thesis prep course (SEIP950) includes "[t]o present tools and opportunities to strengthen research skills" for which I wrote the following learning objective for this course: "Students will create a research log in order to record their search strategies, identifying where and how they have searched (e.g., the keywords and subject terms they have employed)."[79] Once students have identified a topic, the research log directions (Image 3) prompt them to create a concept map utilizing a free mind mapping tool available from the University of Arizona (*http://www.library.arizona.edu/help/tutorials /mindMap/*).[80] Concept maps are great for brainstorming and can serve as performance assessments.[81]

The research log calls upon students to move beyond the mere mechanics of searching in order to reflect on their experiences and grow, thereby embodying the seminary's focus on knowledge, skills, and being.[82] As I created the research log exercise, I solicited input from both the dean of the seminary and the director of the MATS program. My goal with this frame involves students maintaining a research log throughout the semester.[83]

During library sessions for students in the thesis prep course in both the fall of 2017 and 2018, I distributed the research log exercise. Initially, I was hopeful that these logs would be completed and returned to me. However, that has not happened yet. In the future, I plan to revisit this request.[84]

Librarians at other institutions have been more successful in gathering and analyzing research log data. For example, at the University of Tennessee, librarians assess detailed research logs as part of their curriculum mapping.[85] At

Colgate University, students complete a prefocus essay "identifying resources consulted, search terms tried, search strategies attempted, etc."[86]

Research Log Recommendations

1. What is your research topic?
2. Brainstorm with the University of Arizona's mind mapping feature (http://www.library.arizona.edu/help/tutorials/mindMap)
3. Where did you find information (online library catalog, database, etc.) Be as specific as possible
4. For each search tool (online library catalog, database, etc.) describe your search strategy. What keyword did you use? How many search results did these terms yield? Indicate with a plus (+) or minus (–) the relevance of these results.
5. What subject terms did you use? How many search results did these terms yield? Indicate with a plus (+) or minus (–) the relevance of these results.
6. Describe special search features/approaches you used to find information (e.g., scripture citation in ATLA religion database, citation searching, etc.) Indicate with a plus (+) or minus (–) the relevance of these results.
7. How did you broaden or narrow your search results? It may be helpful to visualize your topic as fitting on the rung of a ladder and choose different terms to move up or down on the ladder to narrow or broaden your search results.
8. What "limiters" did you use (e.g., peer-reviewed)?
9. Reflection: How did you determine whether or not your search strategy was effective? How will this impact your searching in the future?
10. Include citations for sources you may use.

IMAGE 3 - Research Log Exercise

Additional Applications

Keeping a research log requires persistence, a skill that librarian Janet Hauck explored by collaborating with four theology faculty at Whitworth University. Hauck received a grant from the Wabash Center for Teaching and Learning that focused research on students' intellectual tenacity.[87] At the beginning of the semester, Hauck met with classes for approximately ten minutes to discuss this concept. She began with the icebreaker: "What is one thing you are good at?"[88] She used this conversation starter to emphasize the importance of hard work and perseverance when it comes to research, which maps to both Research as Inquiry and Searching as Strategic Exploration.[89]

Search exercises, handouts, worksheets, etc. often map to the frame Searching as Strategic Exploration and can easily be adapted for use with multiple populations. The research prescription that I developed for individual appointments with seminary students is a perfect example. I use this worksheet when meeting with both seminary and undergraduate students and believe that it assists students in playing a more active role in learning. Inspired by a similar exercise developed by Fenwick Library at George Mason University, the research prescription prompts students to brainstorm search terms and record where they are searching, similar in some aspects to the search strategy form and research log exercises used with specific seminary courses.[90] Furthermore, I modified the research prescription to serve the needs of undergraduate honors students, who are required to meet with a librarian for approval of their project. While meeting with a librarian, the student completes the form and can refer to it at a later time if desired.

Expanding curriculum mapping to undergraduate programs at Moravian College, the focus centers on the frame Searching as Strategic Exploration. Since the freshman seminar includes a required information literacy session, the instruction librarians decided to map this frame to a handful of specific upper level courses, hoping to expand the scope of information literacy instruction. This new project began in the fall of 2018. Now, each librarian selects at least one course per semester for which she will be leading a library session; so far, classes include the following disciplines: art, English, health sciences, neuroscience, nursing, and psychology. Similar to the curriculum mapping for the seminary, my colleagues and I began by mapping the frames to the college's strategic plan pillars: "academic excellence and innovation, growth through partnership, a culture of community, enroll and retain students and engage alumni, and entrepreneurial stewardship."[91] We then created a tab in Google sheets for each course, mapping course objectives and assignments listed in syllabi to the ACRL frames, as well as the college's pillars. Through this project, my colleagues and I would like to demonstrate that librarians contribute to the learning goals not only of specific courses but also of the institution as a whole. Librarians at Concordia College have found it helpful to align instruction statistics with the frames, and Moravian's library instruction statistics are similarly mapped to the frames, which should prove useful in identifying future collaborations.[92] Since the undergraduate curriculum mapping project at Moravian is still in its infancy, we are still determining the scope of this project and have yet to develop assessment measures.

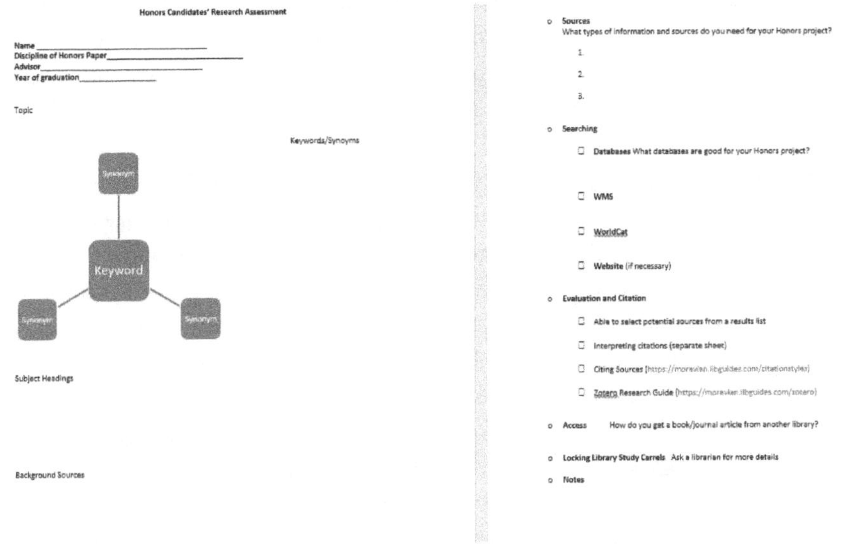
Honors Candidates' Research Assessment

Name ____________
Discipline of Honors Paper ____________
Advisor ____________
Year of graduation ____________

Topic

Keywords/Synoyms

Keyword

Subject Headings

Background Sources

- Sources
  What types of information and sources do you need for your Honors project?
  1.
  2.
  3.
- Searching
  - ☐ Databases What databases are good for your Honors project?
  - ☐ WMS
  - ☐ WorldCat
  - ☐ Website (if necessary)
- Evaluation and Citation
  - ☐ Able to select potential sources from a results list
  - ☐ Interpreting citations (separate sheet)
  - ☐ Citing Sources (https://moravian.libguides.com/citationstyles)
  - ☐ Zotero Research Guide (https://moravian.libguides.com/zotero)
- Access How do you get a book/journal article from another library?
- Locking Library Study Carrels Ask a librarian for more details
- Notes

IMAGE 4 - Undergraduate Honors Appointment Form

Marketing and Outreach

Regardless of the stage of curriculum mapping, this approach can serve as a marketing tool for information literacy. However, in order to be marketable, curriculum mapping must be relevant. Therefore, tying the frames to the curriculum and existing assignments is a great place to start. At the University of Tennessee, teaching faculty received "targeted course maps" indicating how the library assists with both individual courses and entire degrees.[93] Additionally, curriculum mapping is useful for accrediting bodies.[94] Section 4.2 of Moravian's ATS Self Study specifically mentions the curriculum mapping related to the MATS degree.[95]

The perception of librarians can impact the faculty's reception to information literacy curriculum mapping. As a result, library outreach to faculty is imperative for charting a good course. Certainly there is a place for librarians in new faculty orientation to alert faculty of key resources and available services,[96] but the education should not end here. For additional workshops to be successful, libraries could consider providing food and conducting a survey to determine timing and content. Similar to working with traditional students, the sessions should be planned to coincide with times that faculty will be working on research and/or revising assignments. As an example, librarians at Northwest Vista College have gotten it right: during a faculty development seminar they offered a presentation entitled "Top 10 Things," highlighting how faculty can assist students with library research.[97] Additionally, librarians at Northwest Vista offered a lunchtime session on multidisciplinary databases, timing this presentation during an in-service week.[98] Melody Layton McMahon encourages librarians to serve as "'teachers to the teachers.'"[99] Acting on her advice and with the blessing of the dean of the seminary, I offered an information literacy session for seminary faculty in May 2016. In order to make the content as meaningful as possible, I created a survey to gauge awareness of and interest in resources and services. The resulting information literacy session focused on library resources for the new chaplaincy program and highlighted time saving features, such as creating research alerts and citation tools like Zotero. Offering on-point workshops for faculty opens the door for library sessions for students.

Another structured way to reach faculty involves planned visits. At Northwest Vista College, "becoming known on campus" includes offering "office calls."[100] During my first semester at Moravian, I offered something similar, dubbed "house calls." In the fall of 2015, I met one-on-one with any interested seminary faculty members.[101] Not only did I want to get a better sense of faculty members' courses and research interests, but I also was interested in hearing what the library was doing well and how our services could improve. Additional topics of conversation included library instruction and assessment.[102] During one of these meetings, I met with the then-director of the MATS program, and I would like to think that this conversation persuaded him to include library instruction in *Introduction to New Testament* because, historically, library instruction was absent from this course.[103] He also was receptive to assisting with the curriculum mapping project. Since I last offered "house calls" over three years ago, a lot has changed. For one, there are new faculty at the seminary. It is likely time to revisit this mode of outreach, perhaps focusing on the topic of curriculum mapping. Librarians agree that curriculum mapping serves as a great "conversation starter."[104]

Outreach can occur in many forms, and informal conversations should not be underestimated. Librarians at Northwest Vista College highlight the value of visibility at campus events and the conversations that ensue as a result.[105] Certainly, being present at faculty meetings, chapel, and luncheons, as well as offering office hours in the community gathering spot–the seminary's kitchen–one afternoon a week, have worked in my favor. In these settings, I am often asked questions. Students follow up with research appointments, and faculty schedule library sessions. Offering research assistance in satellite locations serves as a form of outreach.[106]

Once faculty recognize that librarians are approachable and eager and willing to support the goals of an institution, the path clears for discussions surrounding curriculum mapping. Nonetheless, it is essential to model open communication and to gain buy-in from faculty and administrators.[107] Presenting curriculum mapping in an easy-to-understand format free of library jargon seems most effective.[108] Curriculum mapping should be an ongoing conversation, sharing updates with key stakeholders.[109] I have done my best to provide progress reports to the dean of the seminary and would like to engage in more brainstorming in the future. Positive change can transpire by sharing curriculum maps with administrators and faculty.[110]

Recommendations

Curriculum mapping is a work in progress, a constantly evolving document that changes with the curriculum; therefore, it needs to be flexible.[111] Accounting for changes in faculty also factors into the equation.[112] Certainly this has been the case at Moravian. When I began working on this project, I worked closely with the director of the MATS program; however, he is no longer at Moravian, and it is unclear who will be assuming this role in the long term. Therefore, making versatile assessments and exercises that can easily be repurposed and retooled saves time and energy.[113]

Curriculum mapping can be labor-intensive, so before embarking on such a project it can be helpful to consider who will participate in the endeavor, as well as the time commitment such a project may entail. Developing a timeline may help with visualizing the project.[114] Starting with a single class is not unreasonable; this is the approach my colleagues and I are taking with the undergraduate program. Regardless of the approach taken, mapping the ACRL frames to valuable institutional measures, such as strategic plan initiatives or an institution's mission statement, will make for smoother sailing and entice key stakeholders to join you on the voyage.

Future Course for Moravian

Curriculum mapping demonstrates the value of libraries as learning partners, for it can highlight contributions librarians make to the curriculum, and this serves as my ultimate goal. With clear links to institutional goals, curriculum mapping also results in a marketing tool and a means of faculty collaboration, efforts I plan to continue. Certainly scholarship informed my project and, as I chart the next course, it will continue to shape the future of curriculum mapping at Moravian. Beginning with the MATS program, I linked gating assessments and course objectives to each of the ACRL frames. In the past, my efforts have concentrated on *Introduction to New Testament* and the thesis prep course, looking for application in the undergraduate program. Moving forward, I would like to shift the focus slightly to account for changes in faculty and the seminary's curriculum. Next, I would like to concentrate on mapping the frames to courses required of all seminary degree programs, hopefully reaching more students and maximizing my impact. The next phase of curriculum mapping will take time; however, repurposing some current information literacy assessments will aid in this process. I plan to start with LinC, a course that all seminary students will now be required to take during their first semester. Already, the dean and I are brainstorming what the revised curriculum may look like and imagine that I will be fully embedded in this course. Within LinC, I hope to provide customized library instruction for each degree program and, as a result, to work more closely with the teaching faculty. The proposed revisions will also provide opportunities for assessment. Once this course materializes, I will look for ways to collaborate with librarian colleagues to model and replicate information literacy training and assessment for undergraduates. The path forward will create new channels for curriculum mapping with numerous possibilities–onward I go!

Bibliography

Archambault, Susan Gardner and Jennifer Masunaga. "Curriculum Mapping as a Strategic Planning Tool." *Journal of Library Administration* 55, no. 6 (2015): 503–19.

Association of College and Research Libraries. *Framework for Information Literacy for Higher Education.* Chicago: American Library Association, 2016.

Association of College and Research Libraries Research Planning and Review Committee. "2018 Top Trends in Academic Libraries: A Review of the Trends and Issues affecting Academic Libraries in Higher Education." *College & Research Libraries News* 79, no. 6 (2018): 286–93, 300.

Association of Theological Schools, The Commission on Accrediting. *General Educational Standards.* Pittsburgh: Association of Theological Schools, 2010.

Badke, William. "The Framework for Information Literacy and Theological Education: Introduction to the ACRL Framework." *Theological Librarianship* 8, no. 2 (October 2015): 4–7.

——. "Not Your One-Shot Deal: Instructional Design for Credit Information Literacy Courses." *American Theological Library Association Summary of Proceedings* 57 (2003): 8–18.

Baggett, Kevin, Virginia Connell, and Allie Thome. "Frame by Frame: Using the ACRL Framework for Information Literacy to Create a Library Assessment Plan." *College & Research Libraries News* 79, no. 4 (2018): 186–9, 200.

Buchanan, Heidi, Katy Kavanagh Webb, Amy Harris Houk, and Catherine Tingelstad. "Curriculum Mapping in Academic Libraries." *New Review of Academic Librarianship* 21 (2015): 94–111.

Bullard, Kristen A. and Diana H. Holden. "Hitting a Moving Target: Curriculum Mapping, Information Literacy and Academe." *LOEX Conference Proceedings* (2006): 17–21. *https://bit.ly/2H6Qrxs.*

Buell, Jesi and Lynne Kvinnesland. "Exploring Information Literacy Assessment: Content Analysis of Student Prefocus Essays." *College & Research Libraries News* 79, no. 11 (2018): 598–600, 606.

Bussert, Leslie. "Marinated in Information Literacy: Using Curriculum Mapping to Assess the Depth, Breadth, and Content of Your Embedded Instruction Program." In *The Embedded Librarian's Cookbook,* edited by Kaijsa Calkins and Cassandra Kvenild, 145–9. Chicago: Association of College and Research Libraries, 2014.

Cuevas, Nuria M., Alexei G. Matveev, and Marvin D. Feit. "Curriculum Mapping: An Approach to Study the Coherence of Program Curricula." *The Department Chair* 20, no. 1 (Summer 2009): 23–6.

Gessner, A., Gabriela Castro, and Erin Eldermire. "Laying the Groundwork for Information Literacy at a Research University." *Performance Measurement and Metrics* 16, no. 1 (2015): 4–17.

Gragg, Douglas L. "Information Literacy in Theological Education." *Theological Education* 40, no. 1 (2004): 99–111.

Harden, R. M. "AMEE Guide No. 21: Curriculum Mapping: A Tool for Transparent and Authentic Teaching and Learning." *Medical Teacher* 23, no. 2 (March 2001): 123–37. *https://doi.org/10.1080/01421590120036547.*

Hauck, Janet. "Crossroads of Mind and Heart: Incorporating Intellectual Tenacity into an Information Literacy Program." *Christian Librarian* 58, no. 2 (May 2015): 95–102.

Jacobs, Heidi Hayes. *Getting Results with Curriculum Mapping*. Alexandria, VA: Association for Supervision and Curriculum Development, 2004: v. Quoted in Heidi Buchanan, Katy Kavanagh Webb, Amy Harris Houk, and Catherine Tingelstad. "Curriculum Mapping in Academic Libraries." *New Review of Academic Librarianship* 21 (2015): 95.

Jenkins, Philip. *The New Faces of Christianity: Believing the Bible in the Global South*. Oxford: Oxford University Press, 2006. Cited in John B. Weaver, "New Faces, New Readers: Uses of the Book in the 'next Christendom.'" *American Theological Library Association Summary of Proceedings* 62 (2008): 234–46.

Kuglitsch, Rebecca Z. and Peggy Burge. "Beyond the First Year: Supporting Sophomores Through Information Literacy Outreach." *College and Undergraduate Libraries* 23, no. 1 (2016): 79–92.

Lincoln, Timothy D. "Curricular Information Demand in Theological Degrees: Operationalizing a Key Concept for Library Services." *Journal of Religious and Theological Information* 12, no. 1–2 (2013): 13–28. *https://doi.org/10.1080 /10477845.2013.794649*.

Lowe, M. Sara, Char Booth, Alexandra Chappell, Sean M. Stone, and Natalie Tagge. "Visual Curriculum Mapping: Charting the Learner Experience." *Library Staff Publications and Research* (2013). *https://scholarship.claremont .edu/library_staff/18/*.

Machovec, George. "Trends in Higher Education and Library Consortia." *Journal of Library Administration* 57, no. 5 (2017): 577–84.

McMahon, Melody Layton. "Librarians and Teaching Faculty in Collaboration: New Incentives, New Opportunities." *Theological Education* 40, no. 1 (2004): 73–87.

Miller, Elizabeth Young. "Connecting and Collaborating with Faculty through Curriculum Mapping." *American Theological Library Association Summary of Proceedings* 72 (2018): 219–29. *https://doi.org/10.31046/proceedings.2018.38*.

Moravian College. "2015–2020 Strategic Plan." Approved by the Joint Board of Trustees January 23, 2015. *https://bit.ly/2XKP2Sg*.

Moravian Theological Seminary. "ATS Self Study." 2017.

Oakleaf, Megan. "A Roadmap for Assessing Student Learning Using the New Framework for Information Literacy for Higher Education." *The Journal of Academic Librarianship* 40 (2014): 510–14.

——. "Writing Information Literacy Assessment Plans: A Guide to Best Practice." *Communications in Information Literacy* 3, no. 2 (2009): 80–9. Cited in A. Gabriela Castro Gessner and Erin Eldermire, "Laying the Groundwork for Information Literacy at a Research University." *Performance Measurement and Metrics* 16, no. 1 (2015): 5.

Reeves, Linda, Catherine Nishimuta, Judy McMillan, and Christine Godin. "Faculty Outreach." *The Reference Librarian* 39, no. 82 (2003): 57–68.

Rudin, Phyllis. "No Fixed Address: The Evolution of Outreach Library Services on University Campuses. *The Reference Librarian* 49, no. 1 (2008): 55–75.

Saunders, Laura. "Academic Libraries' Strategic Plans: Top Trends and Under-Recognized Areas." *Journal of Academic Librarianship* 41 (2015): 285–91. *http://dx.doi.org/10.1016/j.acalib.2015.03.011.*

Sayles, Jeremy W. "Course Information Analysis: Foundation for Creative Library Support." *Journal of Academic Librarianship* 10, no. 6 (January 1985): 343–5.

Zingarelli-Sweet, Desirae. "Prepare a Way through the Wilderness: Transforming Library Instruction by Mapping the Curriculum." Poster presented at the American Theological Library Association Conference, Long Beach, CA, June 17, 2016.

Notes

1. Dave DeRemer, personal communication with author, March 4, 2019.
2. Elizabeth Young Miller, "Connecting and Collaborating with Faculty through Curriculum Mapping," *American Theological Library Association Summary of Proceedings* 72 (2018): 220, *https://doi.org/10.31046/proceedings.2018.38.*
3. Desirae Zingarelli-Sweet, "Prepare a Way through the Wilderness: Transforming Library Instruction by Mapping the Curriculum" (poster, American Theological Library Association Conference, Long Beach, CA, June 17, 2016).
4. Miller, 220–1.
5. Association of College and Research Libraries Research Planning and Review Committee, "2018 Top Trends in Academic Libraries: A Review of the Trends and Issues affecting Academic Libraries in Higher Education," *College & Research Libraries News* 79, no. 6 (2018): 286–93, 300; George Machovec, "Trends in Higher Education and Library Consortia," *Journal of Library Administration* 57, no. 5 (2017): 577–84; Laura Saunders, "Academic Libraries' Strategic Plans: Top Trends and Under-Recognized Areas," *Journal of Academic Librarianship* 41 (2015): 285–91, *http://dx.doi.org/10.1016/j.acalib.2015.03.011.*
6. ACRL Research Planning and Review Committee, "2018 Top Trends in Academic Libraries," 287, 289; Saunders, 285–6.

7. Timothy D. Lincoln, "Curricular Information Demand in Theological Degrees: Operationalizing a Key Concept for Library Services," *Journal of Religious and Theological Information* 12, no. 1-2 (2013): 14-15, *https://doi.org/10.1080/10477845.2013.794649*.

8. Heidi Hayes Jacobs, *Getting Results with Curriculum Mapping* (Alexandria, VA: Association for Supervision and Curriculum Development, 2004), v, quoted in Heidi Buchanan, Katy Kavanagh Webb, Amy Harris Houk, and Catherine Tingelstad, "Curriculum Mapping in Academic Libraries," *New Review of Academic Librarianship* 21 (2015): 95.

9. Heidi Buchanan, et al. "Curriculum Mapping in Academic Libraries," *New Review of Academic Librarianship* 21 (2015): 95; Kristen A. Bullard and Diana H. Holden, "Hitting a Moving Target: Curriculum Mapping, Information Literacy and Academe," *LOEX Conference Proceedings* (2006): 17, *https://bit.ly/2H6Qrxs*; R. M. Harden, "AMEE Guide No. 21: Curriculum Mapping: A Tool for Transparent and Authentic Teaching and Learning," *Medical Teacher* 23, no. 2 (March 2001): 123-37, *https://doi.org/10.1080/01421590120036547*.

10. Susan Gardner Archambault and Jennifer Masunaga, "Curriculum Mapping as a Strategic Planning Tool," *Journal of Library Administration* 55, no. 6 (2015): 505.

11. Harden, "AMEE Guide No. 21," 123.

12. Archambault and Masunaga, 504; Buchanan, et al., 109; Leslie Bussert, "Marinated in Information Literacy: Using Curriculum Mapping to Assess the Depth, Breadth, and Content of your Embedded Instruction Program," in *The Embedded Librarian's Cookbook,* ed. Kaijsa Calkins and Cassandra Kvenild (Chicago: Association of College and Research Libraries, 2014), 146.

13. Nuria M. Cuevas, Alexei G. Matveev, and Marvin D. Feit, "Curriculum Mapping: An Approach to Study the Coherence of Program Curricula," *The Department Chair* 20, no. 1 (Summer 2009): 23.

14. Bussert, 145.

15. Megan Oakleaf, "A Roadmap for Assessing Student Learning Using the New Framework for Information Literacy for Higher Education," *The Journal of Academic Librarianship* 40 (2014): 512.

16. Oakleaf, "Roadmap," 512. While Oakleaf does not explicitly reference Bloom's taxonomy of measurable verbs, it provides a helpful resource for indexing action language to metacognition.

17. Archambault and Masunaga, 504-5, 510.

Praxis

18. A. Gabriela Castro Gessner and Erin Eldermire, "Laying the Groundwork for Information Literacy at a Research University," *Performance Measurement and Metrics* 16, no. 1 (2015): 5.

19. Buchanan et al., 103–4.

20. Kevin Baggett, Virginia Connell, and Allie Thome, "Frame by Frame: Using the ACRL Framework for Information Literacy to Create a Library Assessment Plan," *College & Research Libraries News* 79, no. 4 (2018): 187.

21. Buchanan et al., 104.

22. Bullard and Holden, 19.

23. Buchanan et al., 101; Bullard and Holden, 18; Gessner and Eldermire, 8.

24. Douglas L. Gragg, "Information Literacy in Theological Education," *Theological Education* 40, no. 1 (2004): 104, 107.

25. William B. Badke, "Not Your One-Shot Deal: Instructional Design for Credit Information Literacy Courses," *American Theological Library Association Summary of Proceedings* 57 (2003): 9; Buchanan et al., 107.

26. Buchanan et al., 99.

27. Archambault and Masunaga, 510–511.

28. Archambault and Masunaga, 511.

29. Megan Oakleaf, "Writing Information Literacy Assessment Plans: A Guide to Best Practice," *Communications in Information Literacy* 3, no. 2 (2009): 80–89, cited in Gessner, Castro, and Eldermire, 5.

30. Association of Theological Schools, The Commission on Accrediting, *General Educational Standards* (Pittsburgh: Association of Theological Schools, 2010).

31. Oakleaf, "Roadmap," 511.

32. William Badke, "The Framework for Information Literacy and Theological Education: Introduction to the ACRL Framework," *Theological Librarianship* 8, no. 2 (October 2015): 7, *https://theolib.atla.com/theolib/article/download/385/1310*.

33. Lincoln, 21.

34. Lincoln, 23.

35. Lincoln, 24.

36. Lincoln, 24.

37. Lincoln, 22.

38. Jeremy W. Sayles, "Course Information Analysis: Foundation for Creative Library Support," *Journal of Academic Librarianship* 10, no. 6 (January 1985): 343.

39. Archambault and Masunaga, 510.

40. M. Sara Lowe et al., "Visual Curriculum Mapping: Charting the Learner Experience," *Library Staff Publications and Research* (2013), *https://scholarship.claremont.edu/library_staff/18/*.
41. Lincoln, 24, 26.
42. Leslie Bussert, 146.
43. Lowe et al.
44. Buchanan et al., 99.
45. Miller, 221-2.
46. Miller, 221.
47. Miller, 223.
48. ACRL, *Framework for Information Literacy for Higher Education* (Chicago: American Library Association, 2016): 4.
49. Philip Jenkins, *The New Faces of Christianity: Believing the Bible in the Global South* (Oxford: Oxford University Press, 2006), cited in John B. Weaver, "New Faces, New Readers: Uses of the Book in the 'next Christendom,'" *American Theological Library Association Summary of Proceedings* 62 (2008): 237.
50. ACRL, *Framework*, 4-5.
51. Miller, 221-2.
52. Badke, "Framework," 6.
53. Miller, 224.
54. Oakleaf, "Roadmap," 512.
55. Baggett, Connell, and Thome, 200.
56. Miller, 224.
57. Miller, 224.
58. Miller, 224.
59. ACRL, *Framework*, 6.
60. Miller, 224.
61. Badke, "Framework," 6.
62. ACRL, *Framework*, 7.
63. Miller, 225.
64. Rebecca Z. Kuglitsch and Peggy Burge, "Beyond the First Year: Supporting Sophomores Through Information Literacy Outreach," *College and Undergraduate Libraries* 23, no. 1 (2016): 86.
65. Kuglitsch and Burge, 80, 82.
66. Kuglitsch and Burge, 89.
67. Kuglitsch and Burge, 80.
68. ACRL, *Framework*, 8.
69. Oakleaf, "Roadmap," 512.
70. Miller, 225.

71. ACRL, *Framework*, 9–10.
72. Miller, 222.
73. Miller, 225.
74. Miller, 224.
75. ACRL, *Framework*, 10.
76. Miller, 227.
77. Miller, 227.
78. Miller, 226.
79. Miller, 225.
80. Miller, 225.
81. Oakleaf, "Roadmap," 513.
82. Miller, 225.
83. Miller, 225.
84. Miller, 225–6.
85. Bullard and Holden, 19.
86. Jesi Buell and Lynne Kvinnesland, "Exploring Information Literacy Assessment: Content Analysis of Student Prefocus Essays," *College & Research Libraries News* 79, no. 11 (2018): 598.
87. Janet Hauck, "Crossroads of Mind and Heart: Incorporating Intellectual Tenacity into an Information Literacy Program," *Christian Librarian* 58, no. 2 (May 2015): 97.
88. Hauck, 99.
89. Hauck, 99.
90. Miller, 226.
91. Moravian College, "2015–2020 Strategic Plan," approved by the Joint Board of Trustees January 23, 2015, *https://bit.ly/2XKP2Sg*.
92. Baggett, Connell, and Thome, 187.
93. Bullard and Holden, 20.
94. Cuevas, Matveev, and Feit, 26; Harden, 135.
95. Moravian Theological Seminary, "ATS Self Study" (2017), 25.
96. Melody Layton McMahon, "Librarians and Teaching Faculty in Collaboration: New Incentives, New Opportunities," *Theological Education* 40, no. 1 (2004): 78.
97. Linda Reeves et al., "Faculty Outreach," *The Reference Librarian* 39, no. 82 (2003): 66.
98. Reeves et al., 64.
99. McMahon, 76.
100. Reeves et al., 62.
101. Miller, 220.
102. Miller, 220.

103. Miller, 222.

104. Buchanan et al., 108; Gessner and Eldermire, 15.

105. Reeves et al., 63.

106. Phyllis Rudin, "No Fixed Address: The Evolution of Outreach Library Services on University Campuses," *The Reference Librarian* 49, no. 1 (2008): 60.

107. Gragg, 102, 104–5.

108. Bullard and Holden, 20.

109. Bussert, 148.

110. Buchanan et al., 108.

111. Harden, 134, 136.

112. Bullard and Holden, 21.

113. Miller, 227.

114. Miller, 227–8.

CHAPTER 6

Scholarship as Conversation

Teaching an Information Literacy Course in a Divinity School Curriculum

KAELEY MCMAHAN, WAKE FOREST UNIVERSITY

*W*HEN THE NEW *FRAMEWORK FOR INFORMATION LITERACY FOR Higher Education* was released in 2015, I was immediately drawn to the frame "Scholarship as Conversation."[1] As a naturally shy introvert, it might seem unexpected to focus on the frame that centers "conversation" so clearly. What I was struck by, however, were the connections and networks that are embedded and implied in the concepts of this frame. As a child, the books that started with a family tree or a map with travel routes highlighted always fascinated me. As a young academic researcher, I was intrigued by the acknowledgements section of a book, seeing the network of scholars who had influenced or helped the author along their path of investigation and writing. As a librarian, I still love these aspects of books, but now citations and footnotes capture my attention. All these are ways in which "Scholarship as Conversation" can manifest in and aid the process of academic research. As an instructor, sharing how to use these resources with my students, and seeing the penny drop when they understand how useful they are, is what animates my teaching.

Since starting my professional librarian career at Wake Forest University's Z. Smith Reynolds Library (ZSR) in 2004, I have taught a combination of introductory and advanced information literacy courses. ZSR has had a robust and popular information literacy program for almost twenty years. LIB100: *Academic Research and Information Issues* is currently offered in fifteen sections each semester. Additionally, we offer a slate of 200-level courses customized for specific disciplines (sciences, social sciences, humanities, business, history) or covering specific information topics (history of the book, archival/primary source research, fake news, Wikipedia, business informatics). As the liaison to the departments of Art, Theatre & Dance, Study of Religions, and the School of Divinity, I helped design and, ultimately, teach the humanities-focused course, LIB250: *Humanities Research Resources & Strategies* four times between 2009 and 2014.[2] By 2015, however, we had yet to propose a graduate-level course and, as the liaison to the School of Divinity, I was interested in offering a research and writing course to help the students in that program.

The course that was proposed to the School of Divinity in 2016 was MIN790D: *Introduction to Research and Writing.* Hilary Floyd, who is an alumna of the School and was working as the Academic Skills Counselor at the time, and I designed the course together. In Fall 2017, we taught MIN790D: *Advanced Research and Writing* to second- and third-year students who were working on significant writing projects or considering applying to PhD programs.[3] These courses were evenly divided in lecture content and assignments between my area of "research" and Hilary's area of "writing." By Fall 2018, Hilary was pursuing a PhD elsewhere, so I taught a revised version of our introductory course, CDS512: *Introduction to Research and Writing.* As I was responsible for the research half of the original courses and the *Framework* pertains most directly to these, I will focus this discussion on the research-oriented lectures, readings, and assignments that comprised the three courses.

Integrating the Framework into Course Design

As of 2015, when I was conceptualizing my portion of the introductory course, all ZSR's undergraduate information literacy courses had been designed to meet the criteria of the *Information Literacy Competency Standards for Higher Education* (*Standards*), which had been released in 2000. Designing the MIN790D: *Introduction to Research and Writing* course was, therefore, my first opportunity to implement the concepts and ideas delineated by the updated *Framework for Information Literacy for Higher Education* (the *Framework*).[4] For practical purposes, the *Standards* presented discrete skill sets that were frequently characterized as a checklist of tasks that students should be able to accomplish after information literacy instruction. The *Framework*, on the other hand, highlights the overlapping mindsets and "dispositions" (clusters of preferences, attitudes, capabilities realized in a particular way) that researchers in our current, messier, information landscape need to develop both as users and creators of information. As students begin to absorb these framework concepts and apply them to their research approaches, in addition to mastering specific research tasks, they hopefully will begin to integrate these concepts into a holistic research mindset.

But why focus on "Scholarship as Conversation"? While clearly all the frames are important and contribute to an understanding of the overall task of research, "Scholarship as Conversation" fits most closely to skills and approaches that I already tend to highlight in my teaching. In addition to being the disposition that I believe the students I teach need most, this is the frame that prioritizes citations and crediting the work of others. Correctly citing sources, and even committing inadvertent plagiarism, continues to be an issue for many students in our program, as well as for Wake Forest students as a whole. The main research assignments in the course require students to "critically evaluate contributions made by others" and "identify the contribution that particular articles, books, and other scholarly pieces make to disciplinary knowledge."[5] By "[d]eveloping familiarity with the sources of evidence, methods, and modes of discourse in the field," students also learn to appreciate the variety of scholarly apparatuses that have been constructed over time to assist them in interpreting and connecting to information sources, as well as the fact that there are potential sources *beyond* the traditional book or journal article.[6] This frame also acknowledges the complicated reality of both the collegiality of the academy *and* the ways in which insiders may create roadblocks for those in an outsider position, but it also encourages participation, especially as a student, in the venues that are open to them. And critically, this frame also values ambiguity and the uncomfortable idea that there may not be one right answer; that we are "entering into an ongoing scholarly conversation and not a finished conversation."[7] In a discipline that has been wrestling with its essential questions for millennia, this can have a powerful resonance.

While it was my priority to center "Scholarship as Conversation," the frames are overlapping enough to make it impossible to look at any one of them individually or in isolation. One can't teach a course on research without thinking about the ideas within "Research as Inquiry" or "Searching as Strategic Exploration." Beyond these important research-related aspects, our students are in a professional school and in training to become an authority figure for a faith or community group or a scholar in the discipline and, as a result, frames like "Authority is Constructed and Contextual" become more significant to understand and internalize. As with the overarching theme of "Scholarship as Conversation," elements from each of the frames were incorporated in the course via readings, in-class exercises, lectures, and assignments.

Course Logistics: Readings, Lectures, and In-class Exercises

Because each course consisted of seven to eight class sessions, half of which were devoted to the writing portion of the course, there were only the equivalent of three class sessions that exclusively focused on research. In each of these class sessions I tried to incorporate three elements: a lecture that included an overview of any assigned readings, some type of interactive exercise, and a demonstration of the research skills that the students would need to complete the assignment connected to that day's resource type.

The assignments for the research portion of each course were based on the traditional pathfinder project. Each student selected a topic, usually history- or theology-related, and was then required to find three resources related to that topic. For the introductory course that included a reference resource, a scholarly book, and a scholarly journal article. For the advanced course, I wanted the students to discover types of resources that might be less familiar or use familiar resources in a new way, so the resource categories were slightly different:

- an online reference resource (Oxford Biblical Studies Online, Routledge Handbooks Online, etc...) OR a scholarly non-monograph book resource (collected/edited volume, Festschrift, etc...)
- a book or literature review of at least three books on a topic OR an in-depth interview with a scholar(s) OR scholarly conversations via response articles OR a theme issue of a journal
- a primary source (anthology, critical edition, etc...) OR an archive/special collection/digital humanities project

The final project for the introductory course required the students to make corrections to their three resource assignments and resubmit them along with an introductory scope note and concluding "lessons learned" summary. The advanced course students submitted a final reflection essay discussing the development of their research and writing process but no corrected assignments.

Course Readings

The required citation style guide for the School of Divinity is *A Manual for Writers of Research Papers, Theses, and Dissertations* (Turabian 8th and/or 9th editions), so it made sense to make it one of the required texts for the course.[8] Beyond the citation rules and examples in Part II of Turabian 8/9, I found the research and writing chapters in Part I were so helpful that I ended up assigning most of them when I taught the Fall 2018 iteration of the *Introduction* class, including the "Note to Students" and the "Preface." Additionally, I referred students to Part III ("Style") to answer common grammar and usage questions. These chapters were especially helpful for building confidence in students who had been away from academia for many years or who had not taken writing-intensive courses as undergraduates.

Two of the assigned sources, Turabian 8/9 and *Reading Theologically,* communicated aspects of the *Framework* particularly well, and I was able to reinforce those ideas from the readings by projecting selected quotations and summaries during my lectures. In "Reading Basically," as Melissa Browning introduced the act of reading as a new divinity student, she passed along this wisdom from one of her own professors, "You must dialogue with the [biblical] text... Then, when you think you understand it, when you've dialogued with the text, that's when you should set a circle of chairs and invite the scholars you are reading to join your conversation."[9] This is such a helpful and powerful visual of "Scholarship as Conversation" for students to have as they begin to engage with the various authors and thinkers they will encounter as divinity students! In addition to using and illustrating the phrase "threshold concepts," Browning emphasized that, "we must learn to read in a way that is embodied, communal, spiritual, and transformative in practice."[10]

Chapter One of Turabian 9 began with a similar visualization of "What Research Is":

> *When we walk into a library, we are surrounded by more than twenty-five centuries of research. When we go on the internet, we can read the work of millions of researchers who have posed questions beyond number, gathered untold amounts of information from the research of others to answer them, and then shared their answers with the rest of us. We can carry on their work by asking and, we hope, answering new questions in turn.*[11]

Several pages later, Turabian 9 continues to emphasize the conversational aspect of research, "And when you report your own research, you add your voice and hope that other voices will respond to you, so that you can in turn respond to them. And so it goes."[12] One of my goals in highlighting this conversational view of research is that it can help to take away some of the negative pressure students experience surrounding citations. By framing citations as the act of acknowledging someone else's contribution to a conversation you are having, I hope to mitigate the idea that citations are onerous or only the way that students "prove" that they have done their work.

Beyond "Scholarship as Conversation," Turabian 9 also touched on various elements of the remaining five frames throughout the first two chapters. For example:

- Information Has Value: "Governments spend billions on research, businesses even more. Research goes on in laboratories and libraries... Research is in fact, the world's biggest industry." [13]
- Information Creation as a Process: "In this book we use research in a specific way to mean a process of systematic inquiry to answer a question that not only the researcher but also others want to solve. Research thus includes the steps involved in presenting or reporting it... you must share your findings and conclusions with others." [14]
- Authority is Constructed and Contextual: "But research doesn't ask for our blind trust or that we accept something on the basis of authority. It invites readers to think critically about evidence and reasoning... it must rest on shared facts that readers accept as truths independent of your feelings or beliefs." [15]
- Research as Inquiry: "...researchers do not merely gather facts on a topic... They look for specific data to test and support an answer to a question that their topic inspired them to ask..." [16]
- Searching as Strategic Exploration: "Research projects would be much easier if we could march straight through these steps... the research process is not so straightforward. Each task overlaps with others, and frequently you must go back to an earlier one." [17]

As I have assigned both the *Framework* and these Turabian 9 chapters as readings for the same class session, these readings have helped reinforce each other.

Across the different iterations of the courses, assigned readings beyond Turabian 8/9 and the *Framework for Information Literacy for Higher Education* have included:

- "Reading Basically," [18] "Reading Meaningfully," [19] and "Reading Critically" [20] from *Reading Theologically* [21]
- "Why Write?" "Beginning and Beyond," and "Reading to Write" from *The Seminary Student Writes* [22]
- "Clutter" and "Unity" from *On Writing Well: The Classic Guide to Writing Nonfiction*[23]
- "Grammar Basics," "Phrases, Clauses and Sentences," "Subjects and Objects," "Verbs," "Making the Parts Agree," and "Modifiers and Connecting Words" from *Working with Words* [24]
- "Clinton Devotional Book Pulled After Publisher Finds Further Instances of Plagiarism" [25]
- "Plagiarism, Privilege, and the State of Christian Publishing" [26]

Praxis

Turabian	Framework
Turabian 8, p. 12-13 "As you do one task, you'll have to look ahead to others or revisit an earlier one. You'll change topics as you read, search for more data as you draft, perhaps even discover a new question as you revise. Research is looping, messy, and unpredictable. But it is manageable if you have a plan, even when you know you'll depart from it."	**Research as Inquiry** — "Research is iterative and depends on asking increasingly complex or new questions…" — "consider research as open-ended exploration and engagement with information" **Research as Strategic Exploration** — "design and refine needs and search strategies as necvessary, based on search results" — "understand that first attempts ast searching do not always produce adequate results"
Turabian 8, p. 24-25 "Once you have at least a question and perhaps a working hyphothesis… you can start looking for the data you'll need to support your reasons and test your hypothesis… Once you have a promising source, read it to find other sources… you'll discover gaps and new questions that only more sources can fill. So while we discuss finding and using sources as two steps, you'll more often do them repeatedly and simultaneously."	**Research as Inquiry** — formulate questions for research based on information gaps or on reexamination of existing, possibly conflicting, information" — "value persistence, adaptability, and flexibility and recognize that ambuguity can benefit the research process" **Research as Strategic Exploration** — "Searching for information is often nonlinear and iterative, requiring the evaluation of a range of information sources and the mental flexibility to pursue alternate avenues as new understanding develops."

TABLE 1 - *Turabian 8* quotations mapped to *Framework* statements

Example of a Complete Class Session

MIN790D: *Advanced Research and Writing*

Class Two: Introduction to Research, Citation Styles, and Plagiarism; Using Specialized Reference Resources and Scholarly Books

For our initial class session, students shared possible research topics and goals for the course and were assigned the first two chapters of Turabian 8, "What Research Is and How Researchers Think about It" and "Moving From a Topic to a Question to a Working Hypothesis." These two chapters, along with the Turabian 8 chapters assigned for Class Two, "Finding Useful Sources" and "General Introduction to Citation Practices," prepared them for our class discussion. I started with a few PowerPoint slide questions, answered anonymously via audience response devices ("clickers"), about what the students considered their strengths and weaknesses regarding the research process to be. Almost 40% of the students felt that their research project strength was selecting a topic, while a huge 75% responded that time management was their weakness. These responses helped Hilary and me to modify our future lecture topics to highlight time management strategies for the students.

Our discussion of strengths and weaknesses led directly into the strategies suggested in the Turabian 8 readings. I included PowerPoint slides with specific quotes from Turabian 8, which mapped to descriptions, dispositions, and knowledge practices of the "Research as Inquiry" and "Searching as Strategic Exploration" frames in order to make connections to the *Framework*, another assigned reading for this class session: [27]

To continue this discussion of the *Framework*, I talked about the four characteristics of threshold concepts and how they are transformative, integrative, irreversible, and troublesome (which I think students recognize from their own experiences in School of Divinity courses) and then discussed the specifics of the six information literacy frames and how they might manifest in our course. [28] By way of a real-world example, they had also read Rev. Emily Heath's *Ministry Matters* column responding to the plagiarism of her work by a well-known pastor, as well as a *Publisher's Weekly* article on the pulling of that pastor's book. [29] This current incident illustrated the very real implications of the "Authority is Constructed and Contextual" and "Information Has Value" frames, as well as put them into a context the students could imagine themselves being in. In her column, Heath discussed the struggles she encountered in finding a publisher for her work, based mostly on her identity rather than the content or ideas represented in her writing. She also shared how demoralizing it was to see those same ideas find easy publication when stolen by someone who had more access and clout:

> ...*I'm left with this fact: a man walked into a Christian publisher with my own words—words deemed too controversial for publication—and got those same words published. He took my testimony, and the testimonies of an unknown number of others, and he cashed in on them... When privilege is combined with mediocrity and dishonesty, it's hard not to feel frustrated when it gets rewarded.* [30]

Beyond the obvious plagiarism and citation aspects of this story, it touched on these *Framework* dispositions and knowledge practices and illustrated the interconnectedness of the frames:

– "understand how and why some individuals or groups of individuals may be underrepresented or systematically marginalized within systems that produce and disseminate information" [31]

- "question traditional notions of granting authority and recognize the value of diverse ideas and worldviews"[32]
- "Experts understand that authority is a type of influence recognized or exerted within a community. Experts view authority with an attitude of informed skepticism and openness to new perspectives, additional voices, and changes in schools of thought."[33]
- "The value of information is manifested in various contexts, including publishing practices, access to information, the commodification of personal information, and intellectual property laws."[34]

I finished this portion of the class session by focusing on the "Scholarship as Conversation" frame and the research concepts within it that I wanted the students to understand by the end of the course. This is how I presented these goals on a slide:

- understanding the importance of research and developing ideas based on the work of other scholars
- knowing the required elements of a citation and how to incorporate them into various citation styles
- deciphering various citation styles used in bibliographies to find additional sources
- using clues from footnotes, forewords, dedications, and other scholarly apparatus to understand scholarly networks and methodological approaches
- branching out into other disciplines to create new conversations and fill in gaps
- participate in conferences, contribute to journals, create new sources of information
- be comfortable with ambiguity in approaches and proposed solutions to problems

For the second half of our 90-minute class session, focus turned to the first research resource assignment and the skills the students would need to complete it. I prefer to combine the demonstration of these research skills, which are usually limited to pointing and clicking in the library catalog or database, with some opportunity for students to physically turn the pages of books and examine the types of resources I expect them to find. This usually means that I will wander around in the stacks, collecting a booktruck full of examples for the various categories of resources that I want the students to be aware of. With this particular assignment, students were asked to choose between two types of specialized resources, one of which consisted mostly of online resources and was thus demonstrated mostly through pointing and clicking, and the other that was mostly print and thus could benefit from physical examples:

- Specialized Reference Resource: options included Oxford Biblical Studies Online, Oxford Bibliographies Online, Routledge Handbooks Online
- Specialized Scholarly Book Resource: options included Festschriften, edited volumes, and handbooks or companions

While demonstrating the catalog searches that would aid in finding a Festschrift, or how to read a catalog record to see if it is an edited volume, we looked at the physical books I had pulled from the stacks to see the specific features of these resources and why they can be particularly helpful for a researcher in a given field. When looking at the Festschriften, we discussed:

- why such works are published
- how they represent the impact of an individual scholar on a discipline
- their network of students, colleagues, and mentees
- that biographical, methodological, and bibliographical information on the honoree may be included

For edited volumes and handbooks or companions, we explored:

- that in an introduction or foreword, the editor will explain the organizing theme or approach of a volume and frequently will describe how the individual chapters are in conversation with each other
- how the volume may be the result of a symposium, conference, or series
- that important visual information such as timelines, maps, or charts may be included

After our discussion of how to find these resources and the variety of information they included, I ended the lecture by walking the students through how to write a citation for an edited volume and how it differs from that of a regular monograph.

Examples of In-Class Exercises for CDS512: Introduction to Research and Writing

Class 3: Introduction to Citation Styles and Plagiarism Issues; Using Reference Sources

As part of my lecture on citations and plagiarism, I included slides with excerpts from an article by Margaret Miles, "Mapping Feminist Histories of Religious Traditions," to illustrate the various ways in which quotations or concepts taken from a source can be incorporated into writing, using the guidelines set out in Turabian 9's section 7.4–7.5.[35]

Options for incorporating research...

- **quoting directly**
  - phrases, sentences, or paragraphs
  - evidence that supports your claim
  - "words are strikingly original or so compelling..." (Turabian 2018, 44)
  - must use quotation marks if using exact wording from the original source, otherwise it is a paraphrase (and still must be cited!)
  - use a block quotation for more than five lines of text (Turabian 2018, 78)

and present access to those women? As Irit Rogoff suggests,

> Rather than establishing those perceived as missing from the narrative as fully present, it might be of interest to account for the fact that the fragmented, erased, and ephemeral voices are nevertheless there, miraculously clinging to the rock of historical narrative like so many storm-battered mollusks.[15]

Rogoff urges that when feminist historians write about "fragmented, and ephemeral voices" we cannot and should not "robustly reconstitute them."[16] What we can do instead is observe how "without their vague and fragile presence at the margins, the stalwart presences at the center would lose much of their vitality."[17]

Moreover, Rogoff identifies an assumption, pervasive among contemporary

Margaret R Miles, "Mapping Feminist Histories of Religious Traditions," *Journal of Feminist Studies in Religion* 22, no. 1 (2006): 51.

IMAGE 1 - Powerpoint slide illustrating rules for directly quoting a source

Options for incorporating research...

- **paraphrasing**
  - identify the main idea
  - summarize in your own words
    - convey the author's original meaning in your own words
    - should NOT follow the same sentence structure and pattern as the source
      - try to do your paraphrase <u>without</u> looking at the original passage!
  - cite in the sentence with a signal phrase or at the end of the sentence with a footnote (Turabian 2018, 81-82)

Margaret R Miles, "Mapping Feminist Histories of Religious Traditions," *Journal of Feminist Studies in Religion* 22, no. 1 (2006): 51.

their vitality."[17]

Moreover, Rogoff identifies an assumption, pervasive among contemporary feminists, that precludes attentiveness to historical women's socialization according to class, gender, and social location. Twenty-first-century feminist historians' practice of seeking historical women on the basis of current sympathies, sensitivities, and projections, Rogoff writes, is "narcissistic and self-referential." Empathy should not be privileged "as the primary principle of historical analysis."[18] Feminist historians tend to seek historical women who resisted victimization and found ways to achieve distinctive subjectivities and authorization

IMAGE 2 - Powerpoint slide illustrating rules for paraphrasing people who were willing to pay with their lives for religious sensibilities and loyalties in conflict with mainstream orthodoxy must be allowed to question and contradict the triumphal story.

For example, fourth-century Christian movements sustained some amazingly contradictory changes. These included the devastating Diocletian persecution, followed immediately by Constantine's declaration that Christianity was henceforth to be considered a legitimate sect of the Roman Empire; rancorous debates over doctrine; *and* the erection of magnificent and highly decorated church buildings. Toward the end of the century, Christianity became not only a legitimate sect but also the official religion of Empire, effectively authorizing the persecution of dissidents and marginalization of Jews from public life. In the fourth century, women's ministries were prohibited and women's voices forbidden in church choirs. A large ascetic movement protested the Catholic Church's affiliation with imperial wealth, while the Donatist Church in North Africa criticized Catholics' association with a government that had recently persecuted and executed Christians. Unquestionably, a strain of Christianity emerged from the fourth century stronger, more precise, richer in buildings and imperial support, and attractive to a broad range of people. But narrating the fourth century as a story of "gain without corresponding loss" ignores the considerable cost—and the people who bore that cost—of establishing a Christian Empire.

gap!

Writing History — *sub headings*

gap! — New interests and methods, discussed for two decades in the field of history have not, as yet, been fully integrated into the subfields of Church history and historical theology. These interests and methods, however, can facilitate examination of women's roles in the history of Christian movements. Postmodernism has stimulated diverse new approaches to historical writing as historians' interests have expanded from a focus on wars and institutions to encompass "virtually every human activity."[2] Everyday experience, mental habits, and social arrangements, as well as the politics of interpretation, have come under scrutiny

methodologies as feminist, Marxist, and populist historians explore the past. Moreover, the dissolution of boundaries dividing elite *from* popular cultures [and the challenge to the] assumption of [the] superiority of Western ways of thought have changed what is considered historical evidence, suggesting new subject matter [and] additional actors, . . . more inclusive of multicultural viewpoints. Con-

[marginal notes right side:] common or known to the audience, no citation needed

would like a citation here.

p. 70 use ellipses & square brackets to modify a quotation to fit your sentence— but don't change the meaning!

---

[1] Peter Burke, ed., *New Perspectives on Historical Writing*, 2nd ed. (University Park: Pennsylvania State University Press, 2001), 3.

[2] Ibid., 6, 8.

p. 164 - shortened notes rather than ibid.
Burke, New Perspectives, 6, 8.

IMAGE 3 - Example of marked-up page from the Miles article handout, Margaret R. Miles, "Mapping Feminist Histories of Religious Traditions," *Journal of Feminist Studies in Religion* 22, no. 1 (2006): 47.

I also passed out a marked-up copy of the article, which included my margin notes and other markings, as both a continuation of our discussion from the Class Two lecture on how to actively read sources and as an example of the ways that scholars utilize various writing strategies in their work. In multiple places in her article Miles indicated where there were still gaps in the scholarship on various topics, which is something that students should be looking out for, especially if they intend to do advanced research in a particular discipline: "We do not yet have similarly detailed studies for women in societies outside the Roman world."[36] "New interests and methods, discussed for two decades in the fields of history have not," she explains, "as yet, been fully integrated into the subfields of Church history and historical theology."[37] Concerning those approaches, Miles named several methodologies (populist history, New Historicism) and suggested ways in which these approaches might be used to look at Christian history in new ways. In a practical way, Miles was also a good example of an author who used subheadings to organize her text and clearly numbered her points as she moved through key sections of her discussion, which made her argument easy for the reader to follow. I also encouraged the students to incorporate those techniques that they found helpful as a reader, such as subheadings, into their own writing.

Using this article, or similar ones, as an example for students is helpful in several ways. Not only did they get to read a scholar who wrote clearly and well, but they could also see the ways in which she used multiple techniques to introduce quotations and ideas into her writing. Her ideas were complex, yet she didn't rely on jargon-filled terminology, which I think students feel pressure to do as they begin to write academic work. Also, by giving them a copy that is covered in writing and underlining, I hoped to model for them at least one way of having a conversation with a text, how to notice the scholarly "moves" a writer makes, and to see where the author felt there was further research to be done.

Class 7: Footnotes, Writing Process, and Paraphrasing

While we had discussed how to write footnotes and citations in other class sessions, I used this exercise to walk the students through how to read footnotes in the sources they find. Because different publications use different citation styles and have different rules for abbreviations, I thought it might be useful to have the students work on deciphering the footnote sections of two articles and see if they could find the resource in our collection. I handed out three pages from two articles that had extensive footnotes and assigned a footnote(s) to each student, with the instruction to locate the resource(s) in the footnote via our library catalog or databases. I had already checked the resources to confirm we had them in our collection or that they were accessible through our databases and made a list to use as an answer key.[38] I selected these examples as they included a mixture of journal abbreviations, foreign language titles, editions, multi-author works, articles, chapters, and books, which would require the students to do some critical thinking to "translate." I also brought *The SBL Handbook of Style* into the classroom for them to use to look up any journal title abbreviations. [39]

As usually happens when I have done this exercise in one-shot library sessions, some students found this activity straightforward while others found it more difficult. I knew that we had all the items in our collection or access via our databases, so everyone should have been able to find everything in their assigned footnote(s). As a class, we walked through how to locate the items that students had difficulty finding and discussed the different strategies they used. One unexpected comment from a student at the end of the exercise was that a page of footnotes like the one that I had handed out causes him anxiety. Since my view has always been that seeing a page of footnotes is a blessing, it surprised me that someone could see it as a curse! It was an interesting exchange that I had not anticipated when I chose the page simply because it was the most compact format with which to illustrate the exercise! Overall, however, I think it was a good exercise that helped give students the opportunity to search for known items in our catalog and databases, as well as to practice the strategies they need to know in order to interpret citations in a different format than the one they use on a regular basis.

Assignments

All the resource assignments in both the intro and advanced courses were based on the same three components: search process; source citation; source description and evaluation. As representative examples, I've summarized the Reference Resource assignment from the intro course and the Specialized Scholarly Journal Article assignment from the advanced course. Also included here is information on the Faculty Interview assignment and one extra credit option, the Social Media Project.

MIN790D/CDS512: Introduction to Research and Writing Assignment Examples

Reference Source Assignment

Prompt:
Select an appropriate reference source relating to your research topic. This will most likely be an encyclopedia or handbook article, as your resource will need to be substantial enough to evaluate.

Write your search process:

- Where you started (library catalog, database page, reference collection)
- Your search strategy (terms you used, physical place you looked, links you clicked on)
- The results of your search
- Whether you modified your search strategy and, if so, how
- Any difficulties you encountered in your research

Cite your reference source using Turabian 9, Chapter 17:

- Indicate the section(s) you used to construct your citation (i.e., 17.1.8.2)
- You will likely need to use more than one rule to cite your source
- Pay attention to punctuation, capitalization, and spacing

Describe and evaluate your reference source in paragraph form:

- How is it organized? Is the method of organization logical and useful?
- Scope: How comprehensive or specialized is the resource? What is included or excluded? Remember to check the preface or introduction!
- Author or contributors: What information can you find out about the author? What credentials do they have? Is there an editorial or contributing board? What information is included about them?
- Currency: When was the reference source published? Is the research up to date?
- Bibliography: How extensive is the bibliography? Does it include early as well as more recent literature?
- Does it include links or cross-references to additional articles in the resource?
- Special features: appendices, maps, genealogies, images, timelines

- How does this resource help you begin to answer your research question or address your topic?
- How would you incorporate this information into your final paper? Is it simply background information, or is there a specific piece of information that you might quote or paraphrase?

Rationale and Goals:

The purpose of the resource assignments was to give the students the opportunity to: practice their research skills, write different types of citations, and describe and critically evaluate resources for their use in a research project. Within each of these three elements are smaller steps they must master and broader concepts that they need to integrate into their research mindset. These included knowing which citation rules to use based on the source they have found and understanding that reading the introduction or preface of a reference resource will give them valuable information on what is included or excluded, along with the best strategies for using its features. Ultimately, these resource assignments allowed the students to both implement and demonstrate the greatest number of *Framework* principles in one deliverable, including: developing search strategies, writing citations, using bibliographies, assessing authority, evaluating content and contribution, gaining disciplinary knowledge, understanding what resource to use to answer different types of questions, and considering how they intend to use the information they have found.

Outcome:

Generally, the more time we had in class for the students to work on the resource assignments, the better the results were. Frequently students got off-track at the first step of selecting a resource, so if I could approve their resource before they left class, they had a better chance of completing the rest of the assignment successfully. As this was just the first research assignment in the course, students were also at the early stages of applying some of the *Framework* concepts we had been discussing in previous class sessions and so may have had difficulty with tasks such as critiquing resources or evaluating authority.

Faculty Interview

Prompt:

This assignment consists of three parts:

- *Interview.* You will interview a tenure-track faculty member at Wake Forest using the interview template questions. Feel free to add other questions as they come up in the conversation naturally. Do not simply give the interview questions to your interviewee to fill out. These questions are meant to prompt an interactive dialogue in a face-to-face setting.
- *Presentation:* You will give a five (5) minute presentation to the class. In your presentation, address selected points covered in the interview, and include your reflection on the experience:

    - What did you learn that you didn't know?
    - What surprised you?
    - Did the experience give you a greater understanding of research and writing in an academic career?

- *Write-up.* You will also submit a written summary of your interview. This can be a copy of your interview notes or a more formal summary of the interview, but be sure to include your responses to the three questions above.

Rationale and Goals:
The purpose of this assignment was to give the students a view of the research, writing, and service expectations of a faculty member, as well as a greater understanding of the requirements of a doctoral program in theology or religious studies. The question template provided to the students included questions regarding the faculty member's experiences in the discipline, their doctoral program, and tenure-track job searching. I also provided them with questions specific to the resources and topics of the course:

- What scholarly or professional journals do you subscribe to? Have you been a peer reviewer or editorial board member for a journal or other publication?
- What parts of the research process are most difficult for you? Most enjoyable? Has that changed over time?
- What is the research skill you wish your students could improve on? What research skill do you wish you had had as a student?

Outcome:
One goal left unstated above was that I hoped that hearing their faculty reinforce the research and writing strategies taught in the course might give those

strategies greater credence. For the most part, the faculty achieved this, as they emphasized the importance of using bibliographies and shared how useful they have found conferences and associations for building a scholarly network. One professor even stated she "...wishes students would see research as a conversation rather than as a way to confirm their pre-conceived beliefs."

The Faculty Interview was an assignment for the first intro course and the advanced course. While the students in both courses really appreciated the assignment because it gave them the opportunity to have an in-depth conversation with a faculty member, ultimately it seemed to be a more appropriate assignment for the advanced course, which was designed, in part, for students who intended to pursue doctoral studies. For the second intro course, I shifted the Faculty Interview points and class time to other assignments to better meet the needs of that course.

MIN790D: Advanced Research and Writing Assignment Examples

Specialized Scholarly Journal Article Assignment

Prompt:
Locate **ONE** of the following journal article types relating to your research topic:

- – book review or literature review of at least three books on a topic
- – in-depth interview with a scholar/scholars
- – scholarly responses/conversations via article
- – theme issue of a journal

Your resource must be published in a scholarly, peer-reviewed journal, and the review/interview/article must be a minimum of eight (8) pages in length.

In addition to documenting their search process and writing a citation for their resource, students were expected to reflect on multiple questions, a portion of which depended on which category of the four scholarly journal article options their resource represented. Generally, all the students needed to discuss the author's credentials, the article's organization, how current the article was, the scope of the article, and their analysis of what this resource contributed to their topic. Then, based upon the type of scholarly journal article they used, the students needed to answer targeted questions such as:

- *Review.* How did the reviewer integrate the multiple resources being reviewed? What criteria did the reviewer use? Was the review favorable or unfavorable?
- *Interview.* Did the interviewer and interviewee know each other? What did you learn about the interviewee, their methodological approach to the discipline, or their work? Did anything they shared surprise you?
- *Response articles.* Who were the scholars involved in the exchange? Were the articles and responses even-handed or did the authors seem to be vindictive or trying to score points? How many interactions were you able to track?
- *Special or theme issue.* What was the theme of the issue? Was there introductory or explanatory information about the theme? Were the articles the result of a conference or event or were they solicited via a call for papers? Was there a special editor for the theme issue?

Rationale and Goals:

This assignment was created specifically to highlight some of the types of journal resources that students consult less frequently (or are instructed to avoid) when finding sources for regular research papers. These types of resources are, however, the types of resources that academics need to consult as they both build their disciplinary knowledge and understand how experienced scholars in a given discipline communicate. Some ways in which these types of resources could model aspects of "Scholarship as Conversation" or other frames, include:

- Review essay covering multiple books on a topic

  - illustrates different methodological approaches to the same topic
  - shows the development of an idea or discipline over time
  - demonstrates how a specific piece of scholarship can influence the work of others in the field

- Interview with a scholar

  - shows the evolution of the career of one scholar
  - is a reflection on the development of their scholarship and what the work of a scholar looks like
  - describes the role of mentors, dissertation supervisors, or colleagues
  - highlights participation in scholarly associations, on editorial boards, or as a mentor or dissertation supervisor

- Responses or conversations via article

    - illustrates a direct conversation between two scholars with differing views or conclusions on a topic or research question
    - is a venue for the discussion of a current topic in a discipline
    - reinforces the concept that scholarly conversations are continually evolving and that knowledge creation is never "complete"
    - gives a novice researcher the opportunity to observe one way in which scholarly discussions in their discipline are conducted (sometimes this can be a negative example!)

- Theme issue of a journal

    - introduction will usually discuss reason for theme issue and any unifying topic or methodologies that the contributors are bringing to the topic at hand
    - may represent the work of a scholarly association or organization via papers and additional content delivered at a conference, such as awards, scholarships, interview or question-and-answer sessions, association business

Outcome:

Across the twelve students in the advanced course, each of the four types of specialized scholarly journal article options were represented in the submitted assignments. Two students who submitted excellent work can serve as examples of assignments that met my goals. The first student (S. M.) evaluated a review essay, "Who Matters: The New and Improved White Jazz-Literati: A Review Essay" by Guthrie P. Ramsey, Jr.[40] S. M. appreciated the role of the review essay, stating, "The incorporation of and relationality presented by the author in this book review serve as a useful resource in providing individuals with the opportunity to read a synopsis and critique, while holding the various works in tandem with one another [in order to] bolster the central argument presented." Later in his discussion, and in a conversation with me, S. M. indicated that one of his professors had suggested he contact Dr. Ramsey regarding S. M.'s academic work and future studies, and S. M. was surprised by the serendipity of discovering that he had already come across Ramsey via this article. As I remarked in my grading comment, "Scholarship as conversation! In action!"

The second student (E. L.) came to me for assistance in locating response articles on her topic of women in Proverbs. Together we searched the Atla database using the query: (wom* OR fem* OR gender*) AND (proverbs OR wisdom) AND response. In this instance, the first result, Madipoane Masenya's "Searching for Affirming Notions of (African) Manhood in the Paean in Praise of the 'Eset Hayil?: One African Woman's Response to Joel K. T. Bilwul's Article, 'What is He Doing at the Gate?'" actually met the requirements of the assignment as well as E. L.'s research need for her project.[41] In addition to having the title of the precipitating article in the title of the responding article, there was a direct link to that article record within the Atla database in the field "Related Records," making it easy to identify and navigate to the article being critiqued. In E. L.'s assignment, she evaluated Masenya, "I like that the article includes not just what the author did wrong, but *start[s] with* what he did right! From that 'rightness' Masenya restates her case in where the article could be improved. The author does a fantastic job of evenly distributing between critique and concession." She ended her assignment with, "I believe that Masenya herself will be a person who I will be following from now on." Several weeks after the course ended, E. L. reported back to me that because of her familiarity with Masenya from this assignment, she attended an AAR/SBL panel on which she was presenting. E. L. approached Masenya after the panel, engaged her in conversation, and is now in communication with her. This interaction was actually beyond my goals for the assignment and indicated to me that E. L. had really absorbed the dispositions of the "Scholarship as Conversation" frame and was demonstrating them in her academic life.

Social Media Project Extra Credit

Prompt:
Scholars and theologians use social media tools, too! Find a scholar or theologian who is currently active on Twitter, Facebook, or Instagram or has a podcast, blog, or other web presence. Their university or church webpage doesn't count, it will need to be something interactive or not "institutional." What do they post or share? How regularly are they online or posting? What does their profile information say? How do they interact with followers or commenters? Do they use multiple social media platforms? Have they migrated from one to another? **Write a 1–2 page summary of what you discover and learn from what they do online and how you might apply that to your own future scholarly social media use or presence.**

Rationale and Goals:
There were several goals I had in mind when creating this extra credit option. I wanted students to see how experienced scholars interact, in potentially positive and negative encounters, with other social media users. These users could be

members of the general public, engaged lay people, or other academics in their field. I also wanted students to see how the scholarly networks among followers might be positively leveraged. In my own observation of social media usage, specifically of Twitter, I have seen multiple academics at various stages of their careers leverage their network of followers in positive ways:[42]

- ask for favorite resources on a topic, frequently for class preparation or course syllabi
- solicit potential theories or explanations for a newly observed event, activity, or research topic
- share research related travel, site visits, or archives experiences
- discuss pedagogical or methodological approaches
- promote a new book, article publication, or presentation
- share calls for papers or presentation submissions
- decompress after a national/international conference or meeting
- discuss current issues or problems in their discipline or in broader academia
- retweet any of the above on behalf of another colleague in their network
- suggest or "introduce" scholars in disparate disciplines to each other by "@-ing" them in a tweet (or express surprise when two scholars in disparate disciplines already know each other's work!)

By viewing the social media postings and interactions of a scholar and their network over time, I expected that students would begin to appreciate the importance of the scholarly relationships built during graduate programs and at conferences and how social media allows scholars to extend their conversations by building and sharing their knowledge and ideas. I also hoped that they would see social media as a platform that they could use to engage with those working in the field they aspire to join and "recognize that scholarly conversations take place in various venues."[43]

Outcome:
Two students in the advanced course completed this extra credit assignment by following the Twitter feeds of two scholars. E. L. selected Dr. Nyasha Junior (@NyashaJunior) of Temple University and M. S. followed Dr. Wil Gafney (@WilGafney) of Brite Divinity School. E. L. specifically highlighted Dr. Junior's tweets regarding AAR/SBL conference attendance and appreciated her suggestions of which sessions to attend and why. E. L. also noted that Dr. Junior used her feed to share news about "local events, scholarships, articles… anything that would help someone that follows her." M. S. described Dr. Gafney's use of Twitter this way, "She interrogates her followers with provocative questions that

incite powerful conversations on social media. Her posts could be perceived as controversial … but it is an opportunity to create conversations between people and groups that normally do not share space to do so." Both of these students chose scholars who use Twitter very well and quite frequently. They were able to observe the networking and promotion value of the platform and how it might be beneficial or applicable to their own work, as E. L. stated, "I can see myself using Twitter to help with my internship."

Conclusions

"Scholarship as Conversation" continues to be a helpful frame for me as I approach the teaching of research and writing to School of Divinity students. Because community is such an important aspect of theological education, I think it resonates with our students to conceptualize research as an ongoing dialogue in which they are active participants. One of the prompts for the Research and Writing Reflection in the advanced course was to consider whether framing scholarship as a conversation changed their view of either the research or writing process. Two of the students who responded positively in their reflections, A. M. G. and A. A., stated,

> *I have been very selfish about research because I do it for a grade or for my own personal gain. I had removed the spiritual aspect of it and viewed it as an exclusively academic exercise. The writing process should be done with community and for community and it should be done in a prayerful attitude.*

and,

> *Framing 'scholarship as conversation' impacted the way that I view research and writing in a profound way... now that I look at it like that, I don't go into research looking for a right answer nor do I write thinking that I have the right answer. I am beginning to see scholarship as a marathon, not a sprint.*

For me, these comments indicate that these students have in fact internalized the dispositions and knowledge practices of this frame and can now see themselves as contributors to the larger scholarly conversation in theological studies.

Bibliography

Association of College and Research Libraries. *Framework for Information Literacy for Higher Education.* Chicago: American Library Association, 2016.

Association of College and Research Libraries. *Information Literacy Competency Standards for Higher Education.* Chicago: American Library Association, 2000.

Barreto, Eric D., ed. *Reading Theologically, Foundations for Learning.* Minneapolis: Fortress Press, 2014.

Brooks, Brian S., James L. Pinson, and Jean Gaddy Wilson. *Working with Words: A Handbook for Media Writers and Editors,* 8th ed. Boston: Bedford/St. Martins, 2013.

Browning, Melissa. "Reading Basically." In *Reading Theologically,* edited by Eric D. Barreto, 15–30. Minneapolis: Fortress Press, 2014.

Core, Deborah. *The Seminary Student Writes.* St. Louis: Chalice Press, 2000.

Daugman, Ellen, Leslie McCall, and Kaeley McMahan. "Designing and Implementing an Information Literacy Course in the Humanities." *Communications in Information Literacy* 5, no. 2 (2012). *https://doi.org/10.15760/comminfolit.2012.5.2.108.*

Heath, Emily C. "Plagiarism, Privilege, and the State of Christian Publishing." *ministrymatters.com,* September 11, 2017. *https://bit.ly/2U34x9X.*

Land, Ray, Jan H. F. Meyer, and Caroline Baillie. "Editor's Preface: Threshold Concepts and Transformational Learning." In *Threshold Concepts and Transformational Learning,* edited by Ray Land, Jan H. F. Meyer, and Caroline Baillie, ix–xlii. Rotterdam: Sense Publishers, 2010.

Masenya, Madipoane J. "Searching for Affirming Notions of (African) Manhood in the Paean in Praise of the ʾĒšet Ḥayil?: One African Woman's Response to Joel K. T. Biwul's Article, 'What Is He Doing at the Gate?'" *Old Testament Essays* 29, no. 2 (2016): 360–9. *https://doi.org/10.17159/2312–3621/2016/v29n2a10.*

McMahan, Kaeley. "Teaching Academic Research and Writing." *ATLA Summary of Proceedings* (2018): 295–305. *https://doi.org/10.31046/proceedings.2018.98.*

Miles, Margaret R. "Mapping Feminist Histories of Religious Traditions." *Journal of Feminist Studies in Religion* 22, no. 1 (2006): 45–52.

Society of Biblical Literature, ed. *The SBL Handbook of Style,* 2nd ed. Atlanta, Georgia: SBL Press, 2014.

Turabian, Kate L., Wayne C. Booth, Gregory G. Colomb, Joseph F. Williams, and University of Chicago Press Staff. *A Manual for Writers of Research Papers, Theses, and Dissertations: Chicago Style for Students and Researchers,* 8th ed. Chicago: University of Chicago Press, 2013.

——. *A Manual for Writers of Research Papers, Theses, and Dissertations: Chicago Style for Students and Researchers,* 9th ed. Chicago: The University of Chicago

Press, 2018.

Wenner, Emma. "Clinton Devotional Book Pulled After Publisher Finds Further Instances of Plagiarism." *PublishersWeekly.com,* September 6, 2017. *https://bit .ly/2HTCfay.*

Ramsey, Guthrie P. "Who Matters: The New and Improved White Jazz-Literati: A Review Essay," review of *Saying Something: Jazz Improvisation and Interaction,* by Ingrid Monson; *Jazz in American Culture,* by Burton W. Peretti; and *New Musical Figurations: Anthony Braxton's Cultural Critique,* by Ronald M. Radano. *American Music* 17, no. 2 (1999): 205–15, *https://doi.org/10.2307 /3052715.*

Fiorenza, Elisabeth Schüssler. "Reaffirming Feminist/Womanist Biblical Scholarship." *Encounter* 67, no. 4 (2006): 363.

Smith, Julien C. H. "The Construction of Identity in Mark 7:24–30: The Syrophoenician Woman and the Problem of Ethnicity." *Biblical Interpretation* 20, no. 4–5 (2012): 460–1.

Zinsser, William. *On Writing Well: The Classic Guide to Writing Nonfiction,* 7th ed. New York: HarperCollins, 2006.

Notes

1. ACRL, *Framework for Information Literacy for Higher Education* (Chicago: American Library Association, 2016).
2. See the following article for a discussion of the development of LIB250: *Humanities Research Resources & Strategies*: Ellen Daugman, Leslie McCall, and Kaeley McMahan, "Designing and Implementing an Information Literacy Course in the Humanities," *Communications in Information Literacy* 5, no. 2 (April 17, 2012), *https://doi.org/10.15760 /comminfolit.2012.5.2.108.*
3. See the following presentation summary for a discussion of the development of these courses: Kaeley McMahan, "Teaching Academic Research and Writing," *ATLA Summary of Proceedings* (2018), 295–305, *https://doi.org/10.31046/proceedings.2018.98.*
4. ACRL, *Information Literacy Competency Standards for Higher Education* (Chicago: American Library Association, 2000).
5. ACRL, *Framework*, 8.
6. ACRL, *Framework*, 8.
7. ACRL, *Framework*, 8.

8. Kate L. Turabian et al., *A Manual for Writers of Research Papers, Theses, and Dissertations: Chicago Style for Students and Researchers*, 8th ed. (Chicago: University of Chicago Press, 2013); Kate L. Turabian et al., *A Manual for Writers of Research Papers, Theses, and Dissertations: Chicago Style for Students and Researchers*, 9th ed. (Chicago: The University of Chicago Press, 2018). The 8th edition was used for the 2016 and 2017 courses and the 9th edition was adopted when it was published for the 2018 course.

9. Meilissa Browning, "Reading Basically," in *Reading Theologically*, ed. Eric D. Barreto, Foundations for Learning (Minneapolis: Fortress Press, 2014), 15.

10. Browning, 24, 17.

11. Turabian et al., *A Manual for Writers, 9th Edition*, 5.

12. Turabian et al., *A Manual for Writers, 9th Edition*, 8.

13. Turabian et al., *A Manual for Writers, 9th Edition*, 5.

14. Turabian et al., *A Manual for Writers, 9th Edition*, 5.

15. Turabian et al., *A Manual for Writers, 9th Edition*, 6.

16. Turabian et al., *A Manual for Writers, 9th Edition*, 6.

17. Turabian et al., *A Manual for Writers, 9th Edition*, 11.

18. Browning.

19. Miriam Y. Perkins, "Reading Meaningfully," in *Reading Theologically*, ed. Eric D. Barreto, Foundations for Learning (Minneapolis: Fortress Press, 2014), 31–47.

20. Jacob D. Myers, "Reading Critically," in *Reading Theologically*, ed. Eric D. Barreto, Foundations for Learning (Minneapolis: Fortress Press, 2014), 75–93.

21. Eric D. Barreto, ed., *Reading Theologically*, Foundations for Learning (Minneapolis: Fortress Press, 2014).

22. Deborah Core, *The Seminary Student Writes* (St. Louis, MO: Chalice Press, 2000).

23. William Zinsser, *On Writing Well: The Classic Guide to Writing Nonfiction*, 30th anniversary ed., 7th ed. (New York: HarperCollins, 2006).

24. Brian S. Brooks, James L. Pinson, and Jean Gaddy Wilson, *Working with Words: A Handbook for Media Writers and Editors*, 8th ed. (Boston: Bedford/St. Martins, 2013).

25. Emma Wenner, "Clinton Devotional Book Pulled After Publisher Finds Further Instances of Plagiarism," PublishersWeekly.com, September 6, 2017, *https://bit.ly/2HTCfay*.

26. Emily C. Heath, "Plagiarism, Privilege, and the State of Christian Publishing," ministrymatters.com, September 11, 2017, *https://bit.ly /2U34x9X*.

27. ACRL, *Framework*, 1–9.

28. Ray Land, Jan H. F. Meyer, and Caroline Baillie, "Editor's Preface: Threshold Concepts and Transformational Learning," in *Threshold Concepts and Transformational Learning*, ed. Ray Land, Jan H. F. Meyer, and Caroline Baillie, vol. 42, Educational Futures: Rethinking Theory and Practice (Rotterdam, Netherlands: Sense Publishers, 2010), ix–x, *https:// www.lamission.edu/learningcenter/docs/1177-threshold-concepts-and -transformational-learning.pdf*.

29. Heath, "Plagiarism, Privilege, and the State of Christian Publishing," and Wenner, "Clinton Devotional Book Pulled After Publisher Finds Further Instances of Plagiarism."

30. Heath.

31. ACRL, *Framework*, 6.

32. ACRL, *Framework*, 4.

33. ACRL, *Framework*, 4.

34. ACRL, *Framework*, 6.

35. Margaret R. Miles, "Mapping Feminist Histories of Religious Traditions," *Journal of Feminist Studies in Religion* 22, no. 1 (2006): 45–52.

36. Miles, 46.

37. Miles, 47.

38. Julien C. H. Smith, "The Construction of Identity in Mark 7:24–30: The Syrophoenician Woman and the Problem of Ethnicity," *Biblical Interpretation* 20, no. 4–5 (2012): 460–1, *https://doi.org/10.1163 /156851512X643832*; Elisabeth Schüssler Fiorenza, "Reaffirming Feminist/Womanist Biblical Scholarship," *Encounter* 67, no. 4 (2006): 363.

39. Society of Biblical Literature, ed., *The SBL Handbook of Style*, 2nd edition (Atlanta, Georgia: SBL Press, 2014).

40. Guthrie P. Ramsey, "Who Matters: The New and Improved White Jazz-Literati: A Review Essay: Review of *Saying Something: Jazz Improvisation and Interaction*, by Ingrid Monson; *Jazz in American Culture*, by Burton W. Peretti; and *New Musical Figurations: Anthony Braxton's Cultural Critique*, by Ronald M. Radano," *American Music* 17, no. 2 (1999): 205–15, *https://doi .org/10.2307/3052715*.

41. Madipoane J. Masenya, "Searching for Affirming Notions of (African) Manhood in the Paean in Praise of the 'Ēšet Ḥayil?: One African Woman's Response to Joel K. T. Biwul's Article, 'What Is He Doing at the Gate?'" *Old Testament Essays* 29, no. 2 (2016): 360–9, *https://doi.org/10.17159/2312–3621/2016/v29n2a10*.

42. See the following article for some specific social media examples: David Edward Schmersal, Kaeley McMahan, and Gerrit van Dyk, "Back to Basics," *ATLA Summary of Proceedings* (2018), 141–50.

43. ACRL, *Framework*, 8.

CHAPTER 7

Building Competencies

Using the ACRL Framework to Construct an Information Literacy Lab for Undergraduate Students

JÉRÉMIE LEBLANC AND VICTORIA TSONOS, ST. PAUL UNIVERSITY

*I*N 2000, THE ASSOCIATION OF COLLEGE RESEARCH LIBRARIES (ACRL) introduced the *Information Literacy Competency Standards for Higher Education*.[1] After fifteen years, and as scholarship and teaching evolved to meet changing requirements, the *Framework* was developed to meet the new challenges and realities of students' needs. The advent of the *Framework for Information Literacy for Higher Education* in 2015[2] (hereafter the *Framework*) provides academic institutions with renewed mechanisms allowing for a better understanding of fundamental concepts and allowing the information consumer to become an active participant in the creation and use of knowledge. Also in 2015, the library at Saint Paul University (SPU) was asked how it could better support academic student success.

During the summer of 2015, the Chief Librarian (CL) was invited to a planning meeting under the Vice-Rector Academic and Research, during which there was a thorough discussion on how the library could help with student achievement. This discussion focused on librarian instruction for providing students with better research skills and tools to avoid plagiarism. Knowing how information literacy (IL) could play an important role in students' lives during and after their time at university and that the competencies they develop could support them throughout their lives, the Chief Librarian agreed to research ways in which the library could support their students by participating in some way with the core courses offered at SPU.

The arrival of the *Framework* and the request from university administration provided the perfect opportunity to create something new and challenging for the library and something fresh and creative for the students. The HTP courses (Humanities, Theology and Philosophy) were created to provide students with fundamentals inspired through the programs offered at Saint Paul University. Initially there were four HTP courses: HTP1101: *Trends in Western Thought*; HTP1102: *The Artistic & Literary Imagination*; HTP1103: *People, Politics and the Planet* and HTP1104: *Faith, Justice and the Common Good*. The Library's goal was to find a way to collaborate with these HTP courses and implement the teaching of information literacy (IL) skills within them. The *Framework* offered a starting point to examine the various IL needs of students and provides suggestions on how the library could work alongside the HTP courses. From the *Framework*, various concept thresholds were identified as fitting the courses: Research and Inquiry; Searching as Strategic Exploration; Authority is Constructed and Contextual; Information Has Value; and Information Creation as a Process.

To better understand the challenges of this initiative, this chapter will first look at the university's history and the makeup of its student body. This background will be followed by a literature review on the *Framework* and information literacy and then a discussion and analysis on the set-up of the initial pilot project and its growth from conception to full implementation in the fall 2018 semester.

Saint Paul University (SPU) is a small bilingual (French–English) Catholic university located in the heart of Canada's national capital Ottawa. The university's history dates back to 1848, with the founding of Bytown College by the Oblates of Mary Immaculate, and it sits on the grounds of the former university seminary of the University of Ottawa. After the split with the University of Ottawa in 1965, SPU kept its ecclesiastical faculties, those of Theology, Canon Law and Philosophy as well as a handful of programs. These other programs eventually combined to create a new faculty of Human Sciences and Philosophy, which currently has departments in Conflict Studies; Counselling, Psychotherapy and Spirituality; Ethics, Social Justice and Public Service; Social Communication; Social Innovation; and Transformative Leadership and Spirituality. Since SPU is bilingual, courses in each language are commonly offered and students have the right to submit their assignments in either language, not necessarily in the language of the course being offered.

Currently, the University has approximately 1,100 students split roughly 60/40 between undergraduate and graduate students. When the pilot was initiated in 2015, the university only had approximately 750 students. The makeup of the student body was not typical of most other universities, with less than 21% of its students under the age of 24 and only a handful of students coming directly from high school. Since 2015, the number of students coming directly from high school has continued to increase (38 students enrolled directly from high school in 2018). However, as seen in the table below, the university has a significant number of mature students aged 40 or older. At the time the pilot started, they represented almost 45% of the student body, which fell to 34% in 2018 while the number of registered students remained approximately the same. The university has also maintained just under 20% of its enrollment from international students stemming from over 100 countries.

Age group	Fall 2016	Fall 2018
18-24	21%	30%
25-29	14%	17%
30-39	29%	19%
40-49	22%	17%
50+	23%	17%

TABLE 1 - Student enrollment at Saint Paul University by age group (undergraduate and graduate)

Such a diverse student body, in terms of age and linguistic culture, presents a variety of challenges. As noted in the table below, in 2018 the age groups were quite varied. All the same, 59% of these students were adult learners as defined by McCall, Padron and Andrews (students over the age of 24).[3] Depending on the experience, knowledge and access to computers as well as methods of teaching and understanding concepts, for adult learners in particular there could be challenges with digital literacy. Having an approach that welcomes everyone and that is adaptive regardless of his or her experience and background is key to a successful training experience.

Age group	Fall 2016	Fall 2018
18-24	35%	41%
25-29	14%	17%
30-39	19%	17%
40-49	15%	14%
50+	17%	11%

TABLE 2 - Student enrollment at Saint Paul University by age group at the undergraduate level

Multiple factors had to be considered as the training was developed, which focused exclusively in the pilot on undergraduates. Split evenly between French and English, the bilingual student body was non-typical in its range of age groups, in having such a large number of adult learners, as well as in having approximately 16% of the students within the undergraduate group coming from outside of Canada's borders.

Literature Review

With the arrival of the *Framework* in 2015, the interactions and processes around IL instruction have dramatically changed. The *Framework* allowed for "re-envision[ing] … [the] goals of information literacy and fundamentally seeks to help students to understand the knowledge-making process and to strengthen their own facility when it comes to using and creating diverse information or knowledge products."[4] Julia Bauder and Catherine Rod state that the "*Framework* represents a radically different understanding of information literacy" and one premised differently compared with the ACRL *Standards* published more than a decade earlier.[5] Associate Librarian for Information Literacy at Trinity Western University William Badke explains that "librarians and faculty need to work together to determine learning outcomes for various frames and then develop instructional sessions and assignments that will make these genuine threshold concepts … that both create student scholars and enable them to engage in significant research."[6] The *Framework* changes the approach and results, allowing for a more adaptive way of learning and understanding key concepts and research questions. These new concepts were defined in the *Framework* to better address the changing needs of students and to prepare them for the workforce. However, there is no perfect formula and there are varying degrees of success in implementing the *Framework*.

While librarians tend to deliver one-time training sessions or else are invited to courses, on rare occasions librarians can be embedded in courses and play a more significant role in IL. In some cases, librarians are able to work with faculty to conceive plans on how to better integrate the *Framework*.[7] The *Framework* allows for more flexibility when determining outcomes. As Jacobson and Gibson state, the "*Framework* does not enumerate learning outcomes, but offers great freedom for librarians to write their own at their institutions, or to adapt or revise their current IL outcomes."[8] Insua, Lantz and Armstrong at the University of Illinois at Chicago have documented the roadblocks with first-year "students as they struggle with and learn how to conduct research."[9] However, identifying outcomes does not mean success as students face a variety of challenges, and retaining the skills learned without continued practice such as in academic assignments is very important for long-term success. If the concepts are well taught and the students can apply these, there is a chance that they will use these skills throughout their academic and future career(s).

Realizing that there are various challenges that can come from providing embedded undergraduate IL instruction, our institution also had to deal with bilingualism, international students, and adult learners in the mix with regular undergraduate students. In dealing with international students, Susan Avery noted that "adjustments ... [including] class pace and language are important... assignment expectations must be clear and directions for completing them must be given in multiple formats."[10] There are a variety of issues that can arise from international students, some are ESL (English as second language) or FSL (French as second language) students and might have a different understanding of what plagiarism means. Beyond that, as mentioned, the student population at SPU is also varied in age and this presents challenges with andragogy or adult learning. In defining students over the age of 25 as adult learners, McCall, Padron and Andrews also explain that:

> [t]he central tenets of andragogy, as developed by Malcolm Knowles (2012) and based on the original theories of Eduard Lindeman, are: "(1) the learner's need to know, (2) self-concept of the learner, (3) prior experience of the learner, (4) readiness to learn, (5) orientation to learning, and (6) motivation to learn" (p. 3). In the classroom, this translates to a "focus on learning rather than on teaching," and on lifelong learning to where students are taught skills and strategies they can apply to their career(s) and throughout their lifespan (Knowles, 1980, p. 18). These concepts are now familiar to most educators since Lindeman and Knowles' original work, and many recent education studies use the principles of andragogy.[11]

As these concepts are not necessarily new, they cannot be forgotten when instructing students who vary in age. Some of these concepts can also be applied to international learners. Ishimura and Bartlett note that "It does not necessarily follow that librarians are equipped to teach effectively in these circumstances."[12] International students pose a challenge but, by using the concept thresholds from the *Framework* and considering the educational theories around adult learners, there are ways to deliver effective and efficient training. Because of a lack of literature on the subject, it is difficult to determine how students from various demographics respond to IL instruction using the *Framework*. Too often these groups are conflated for analysis, but rarely are they segregated or defined in studies as individual pieces to the bigger picture.

The Pilot

Shortly after the meeting that initiated the call for IL skills for all undergraduate students, the Chief Librarian (CL) met with the Dean of Human Sciences and Philosophy as the Humanities, Theology, and Philosophy courses fell under their responsibility. After an initial discussion, the CL discussed with the program coordinator overseeing the HTP courses how an IL component could be added to the HTP courses. The professor in charge presented no challenges as he saw the benefits and supported the Vice-Rector Academic's decision. As indicated ealier, there are four HTP courses, and each one is offered in French and in English, normally two French (e.g., HTP 1 & 2) and two English (e.g., HTP 3 & 4) are offered during the fall session and then two French (e.g., HTP 3 & 4) and two English (e.g., HTP 1 & 2) during the winter session. The library had to plan out how it would teach to all of these groups. Normally there are approximately 120–160 students in total per semester registered in these courses. The French courses tend to have more students, usually 30–60 per course as the English courses tend to have 25–40 students registered.

As this was a pilot, there was initial brainstorming with librarians over the results. Meeting with the program coordinator, the CL specifically discussed the approach, engaging students, what's the added value, among other topics, while also thinking of strategies to encourage the greatest participation. The librarians along with the CL determined that voluntary IL workshops would provide the best service to the students as well as provide a solid starting point. The library proposed to teach elements through two training sessions one and a half hours in length. Each course was taught by different professors, normally two or three professors sharing the twelve-week semester, each of them teaching four or six classes. This arrangment meant, however, that the library was not allowed to use class time for its instruction. We opted to offer our training sessions during the lunch hour, when no classes were scheduled on campus in hopes of drawing in more students. We also offered the option to do individual one-on-ones with students if they had valid reasons they could not attend lunch hour workshops (e.g., job, medical appointments).

In order to draw students in, the CL suggested that bonus points could be offered to students participating in the training sessions. Initially, up to ten bonus points were proposed for students taking part in the training and completing the assignments. These bonus marks could then be applied to their final grade for the course. The professor in charge of the program was on board with this idea, hoping that we would draw in more participants. However, during the fall 2015 semester only fifteen students out of a potential 120 came to the workshops and completed the assignments. In the winter session, 28 students signed up for the training out of a potential of 130. The class average in the fall was 7.4/10 bonus marks and in the winter session it was 6.7/10.

During the fall 2016 and winter 2017 sessions, students were offered up to 15 bonus points in the hopes of drawing more students to the sessions. During the fall and winter sessions, the number of participants went up to 69 and 51, respectively. Overall, the 2016–17 school year attracted more students, 120 out of a possible 230, drawing over 50% of the students to take part in the IL sessions. The fall average was 9.33/15 and winter average was 7.27/15. We believed that the increase in potential bonus marks attracted more students to participate; however, the overall average is not indicative of the participation. In these calculations, students who just showed up to a training session and never submitted assignments were counted, as we had also allotted points for class participation. The students could have potentially received three points just by going to the two training sessions. The highest mark achieved was 14.4/15.

The pilot project plan was intended to last two years with the goal of implementing these sessions as a mandatory component of the HTP courses for the fall of 2017. However, in 2017 the University's curriculum review came into place and the HTP courses were to be redesigned. This meant that the pilot could continue with the fall session using the current courses or wait for the new courses to be launched in the fall of 2018. The Dean assured the library would not be forgotten in the curriculum review and that an IL component would be fully integrated in the courses. However, with the curriculum review completed, the courses had changed, and the library was offered a new opportunity. The workshops would have to be combined and attached to one HTP course in French and one in English. In order for the library workshops to be integrated into the course, we proposed to teach for ten hours of class time. However, the faculty did not want to release class time. A compromise was achieved by creating a mandatory "library lab" (outside of class hours) to one of the HTP courses that would be divided over ten weeks and last one hour per week. With that, the library would also receive 30% of the final course grade to be attributed through assignments and class participation.

Creating the Course Syllabus

Once the library lab had been approved by the Faculty of Human Sciences, the library began crafting the syllabus (see Appendix 7A). The purpose of the lab was to complement the new HTP critical writing course by introducing basic IL skills to students–an essential component for academic achievement. The *Framework* was then consulted and adapted according to our needs. The *Framework* was adapted to best fit the unique student demographic, the first-year experience as well as the university's focus on humanities and social science programs. As SPU is a bilingual university, content for the different sections of the course created needed to be available in French and English, which meant each assignment, quiz and presentation had to be designed in both languages.

In addition to consulting the *Framework* in creating the syllabus, course structure and assignments, librarians also wanted to highlight the various library services and tools that are offered to students. For many students, a similar course is offered upon entering Saint Paul, but many of these students never set foot in the library and weren't aware of library services, or even aware where the library was located. Integrating information about the services and resources and giving students access to and regular interaction with a librarian on a weekly basis demystified the library and made it a space that students could feel more comfortable using.

In the pilot, different aspects of the *Framework* were explored, which informed the exercises and assignments that were created. For the HTP library lab, the assignments from the pilot were adapted to better follow the structure of the course. In addition to exploring the *Framework's* six threshold concepts, we also explored the librarian's first-hand experiences with students in one-on-one appointments and reference interviews. This was accomplished by examining the students' current IL skills and the need to address these skills with a diverse set of students from different countries, backgrounds and ages. Based on student demographics, the *Framework* suggestions and one-on-one experiences, it was determined that presenting library resources, citations and academic integrity, and evaluation of sources needed to be priorities in this lab.

Once the main concepts of IL were taught, practical applications were examined to incorporate the concepts, such as annotated bibliographies and literature reviews. These were taught more specifically to help students directly with future assignments in other courses and to show how to practically apply what had been taught during the semester. Each of the six concept thresholds were consulted in the pilot and further examined when expanding the pilot for the lab. Special attention was given to the concepts of Authority is Constructed and Contextual, Information Has Value, and Searching as Strategic Exploration, as these concepts aligned well with the IL issues we were seeing in students from across each demographic. The lab also touched upon Information Creation as Process, Research as Inquiry, and Scholarship as Conversation, although to a lesser extent than the other concepts. While these concept thresholds were used as guidelines for the creation of the syllabus, the *Framework* was ultimately used as a guideline and needed to be adapted to prioritize certain concepts for the needs of SPU students. Using the *Framework* helped outline the course and establish a foundation of information tools and strategies to build upon throughout the course and for future in-library workshops.

The Course

The lab was offered over a 10-week period during the fall 2018 semester. This lab was meant to complement and accompany the English and French first-year writing course, also known as HTP1105 and HTP1505. The English course, titled *Critical Analysis, Reading and Writing Academic Works,* focused on establishing critical reading and thinking skills, as well as academic writing. For the library lab, the students were offered the option of choosing one of two one-hour sections. Once organized into two time slots, the first lab enrolled fifteen students with the second having six students. The lab was given in a lecture-style format with various exercises and in-class activities. The lectures were accompanied by presentation slides that were provided to the students on Brightspace (learning management system) after the second lab had finished. In general, students seemed receptive to the course and actively participated in class discussions. While there were no office hours in place for the librarians teaching the labs, students were encouraged to email and make appointments if they ever had any trouble.

The library also integrated the instruction of various tools promoted by the library such as Zotero and Yewno. The library recommends Zotero as a bibliographic management tool, and this was taught alongside citation styles. Yewno is a knowledge mapping tool that we have licensed and that is available through our research guides. This tool was taught alongside mind and concept mapping to help students visualize their research topics and use various tools to aid them with research, making connections between concepts and finding library sources.

Creation of Assignments

The assessment for this lab was divided into four parts (Appendix 7A): attendance and participation, two in-class quizzes, an essay, and an annotated bibliography. Each of these assessed various concepts within the *Framework.* Attendance and participation were considered important given the nature of the subject matter being taught and the value of the in-class exercises. The quizzes were also included to assess students' grasp of basic concepts throughout the course. The first quiz focused on creating a research question and applying search strategies, as well as identifying the different types of sources, while the second focused on citation styles, plagiarism and academic integrity, as well as evaluating sources.

Each written assignment, the essay and the annotated bibliography, was designed to evaluate students' practical application of the concepts taught. For the essay, students were asked to explain why plagiarism was deemed unacceptable in an academic setting. They were required to use no less than three academic sources to support their arguments. The grading rubric for this assignment focused on the students' abilities to properly search and select academic sources, the use of citation styles and their knowledge of plagiarism and academic integrity (see Appendix 7B). The first assignment introduced students to the components of a research paper. For this assignment, students needed not only to demonstrate that they understood the concept of academic integrity, could discuss copyright, and could properly demonstrate proper attribution, but they also needed to demonstrate their research skills in finding peer-reviewed scholarly articles.

The second assignment was an annotated bibliography, which was designed to assess students' ability to take what was taught and apply it in a common assignment. The rubric for this assignment followed a similar pattern to the first. Emphasis was placed on the students' ability to identify the pertinent parts of their article for their needs and to properly evaluate their sources. Correct use of citation styles was given a heavier weight for this assignment, inasmuch as this seemed to be the biggest obstacle for the students. As preparation for this assignment, extra instruction was given on using citation styles.

Results

In general, this lab was well received by students. Students could now benefit from having continuous IL instruction instead of trying to push as much information as possible into a 50-minute workshop. The added element of it being compulsory meant that all students received this training, which helped reduce the gap in IL levels amongst first-year university students. Because of the particular demographics at Saint Paul, students are coming from various backgrounds, ages and knowledge levels. In general, the students verbally expressed that they felt the course was useful and the concepts were important, regardless of their age or previous university experience.

One thing of note was the similar nature of reasons for the significant gap in IL knowledge, whether first-year students coming directly from high school, mature students, or international students. Due to their years of being outside academia, some mature students indicated that they had forgotten many concepts, as well as not being familiar with new tools and online resources. Students coming into university directly from high school as well as international students also expressed that they were not all taught basic IL skills, and their knowledge of online resources beyond Google was limited at best. All students, however, expressed their interest in learning new practices but also felt overwhelmed at the amount to learn. Moreover, the students generally expressed their lack of knowledge of citation styles, properly attributing their sources and finding and evaluating academic sources. When these concepts were introduced, citation styles proved the most difficult for the students to grasp. Practice exercises and examples were then given at the beginning of almost every class for the different citation styles (APA, MLA and Chicago, the three most used citation styles at SPU) to address this issue.

This gap in IL knowledge among different student populations provided one of the main reasons for designing the lab and making it compulsory, evidence of this gap in IL knowledge having been seen in various workshops and courses. Typically, the library offers in-library workshops as well as in-class presentations on demand, but as previously mentioned, one 50-minute workshop cannot adequately demonstrate and teach the various aspects of IL that the *Framework* recommends for students. In addition, many students do not take advantage of the library workshops that are offered each semester. By offering a compulsory lab, we were able to benefit from a traditional classroom setting and assess how the students absorbed and learned these skills.

By being able to evaluate the assignments and interact with students on a weekly basis, the librarians were able to better recognize the difficulties students were having that they weren't able to assess through the in-library workshops. Specific terms, expectations and basics that seemed obvious and straightforward to the librarians were either confusing or unknown to students. It helped the librarians better understand how they needed to adjust not only for this course but also for the future in-class and in-library workshops. Overall, both students and librarians benefited from this lab as it helped to give students a stronger IL foundation and to equip them with skills they might not have necessarily retained in a single 50-minute workshop. It also helped librarians identify the areas in which the IL gaps are greatest and how the library can best adapt and implement changes to further help our students.

Limitations

While the lab was generally seen as a success, moving forward there are some limitations that will need to be addressed to improve the lab for next year. Firstly, the pilot project was put together very quickly. Official approval for the HTP library lab came mid-August; therefore, there was less than a month to prepare a syllabus, assignments and lectures. While elements from the pilot were used to create the lab, the process was still very rushed since it was so close to the beginning of the school year. Along with planning the HTP course, there were also different events and workshops that the library had planned for September, and with a small library staff it was difficult to plan the HTP lab and execute other regular library activities that are done each year.

Another issue caused by the short turnaround period was that the librarians did not have a chance to engage and collaborate with the professors teaching the HTP course. Initial contact was made prior to the course but there was no face-to-face interaction until the course began. There also was no time for collaboration between the course and its curriculum and the lab to ensure that there weren't scheduling conflicts or overlap in content. Librarians were told that the faculty members would base their instruction and class progress on the library lab as indicated in the syllabus. However, librarians teaching the lab did not see the official course syllabus until a week prior to the first class. This not only affected the librarians teaching the lab but also the students as well, as they were asked last minute to add an extra hour of class time to their schedule. This proved especially difficult because each student already had their class schedule finalized, which caused many conflicts when the administration tried scheduling the labs and accounting for student and librarian availabilty. Because at least one of the lab times had to pose no conflict with the students, this was extremely difficult to manage as some students were part-time and were only enrolled in evening classes, while others were full-time and had classes almost every day. Ultimately, the administration was able to find two appropriate time slots for the labs, but this still caused some inconvenience as students found out the first week of class that they needed to incorporate another hour into their weekly schedule. All the same, in their course evaluations students expressed their interest in reading more articles and having more take-home exercises. This was surprising as the lab added an extra hour to their course timetable at the last minute, as well as added extra work. While students did express their displeasure at the last-minute addition to this lab, they also expressed their gratitude and enthusiasm for the lab and understood its importance.

One change to focus on for future labs would be focusing less on the *Framework* and assuring that we meet most of the concepts but instead catering it more to the needs of our students and focusing on teaching lifelong information skills instead of the immediate academic benefits. The focus of this lab was to immediately equip the students with the tools they needed to succeed and complete their future assignments; however it was equally important to focus on how the different concepts being taught could apply to more than just their academic careers and assignments.

Moving Forward

Moving forward, some possible changes and improvements could be incorporating more digital and media literacy instruction in the labs and using better real-world examples outside of academia. Another area for examination is students' own perceived knowledge of research practises and skills before the lab, followed by developing ways to track and assess the progression of IL skills and the impact of the lab on the students. Having a better understanding of what students already know and don't know and how big a gap there is between the knowledge of first-year students from high school, international students and mature students would better serve the wide range of students at SPU. This lab was created to accompany the HTP course to address a need that librarians and faculty were seeing. Continuing to adapt and improve upon this course as well as to collect more data/information on how this course affects students will help not only to justify this course but will hopefully help librarians to integrate similar labs, accompanying lectures or even full courses dedicated to IL and other library instruction.

This lab is currently only offered to undergraduate students enrolled in the HTP1105 and 1505. When the final syllabus was presented to the faculty council in Human Sciences, they expressed their interest in the possibility of the library developing a similar lab for graduate students in the Conflict Studies and Counselling and Spirituality programs. Further discussion and collaboration with these programs will need to address the unique needs of graduate students and how a similar lab can be created for them.

In conclusion, the implementation of a mandatory IL lab helped the library further support the faculty and students of SPU. Further collaboration with faculty will be essential in creating more strategies for IL instruction to support all students regardless of their demographic. Librarians could also benefit from examining the impact the lab has had on students' IL skills and their academic success in order to better adapt instruction. The *Framework* proved an essential tool in the realizing of the pilot project and will continue to be consulted for future IL teaching opportunities.

Bibliography

Association of College and Research Libraries. *Information Literacy Competency Standards for Higher Education.* Chicago: American Library Association, 2010.

Association of College and Research Libraries. *Framework for Information Literacy for Higher Education.* Chicago: American Library Association, 2016.

Avery, Susan. "Setting Them Up for Success: Assessing a Pre-Research Assignment for First-Year International Students." *Communications in Information Literacy* 11, no. 2 (September 2017): 324–38. *https://doi.org/10.15760/comminfolit.2017.11.2.5.*

Badke, William. "DIKTUON: The Framework for Information Literacy and Theological Education: Introduction to the ACRL Framework." *Theological Librarianship* 8, no. 2 (October 2015): 4–7. *https://doi.org/10.31046/tl.v8i2.385.*

Bauder, Julia and Catherine Rod. "Crossing Thresholds: Critical Information Literacy Pedagogy and the ACRL Framework." *College and Undergraduate Libraries* 23, no. 3 (2016): 252–64. *https://doi.org/10.1080/10691316.2015.1025323.*

Fullard, Allison. "Using the ACRL Framework for Information Literacy to Foster Teaching and Learning Partnerships." *South African Journal of Libraries and Information Science* 82, no. 2 (2016).

Insua, Glenda M., Catherine Lantz, and Annie Armstrong. "Navigating Roadblocks: First-Year Writing Challenges Through the Lens of the ACRL Framework." *Communications in Information Literacy* 12, no. 2 (January 1, 2018): 86–106.

Ishimura, Yusuke and Joan C. Bartlett. "Are Librarians Equipped to Teach International Students? A Survey of Current Practices and Recommendations for Training." *The Journal of Academic Librarianship* 40, no. 3–4 (2014): 313–21. *https://doi.org/10.1016/j.acalib.2014.04.009.*

Jacobson, Trudi E. and Craig Gibson. "First Thoughts on Implementing the Framework for Information Literacy." *Communications in Information Literacy* 9, no. 2 (September 2015): 102–10.

McCall, Rebecca Carlson, Kristy Padron, and Carl Andrews. "Evidence-Based Instructional Strategies for Adult Learners: A Review of the Literature." *Codex: The Journal of the Louisiana Chapter of the ACRL* 4, no. 4 (February 1, 2018): 29–47.

Mullins, Kimberly. "IDEA Model from Theory to Practice: Integrating Information Literacy in Academic Courses." *The Journal of Academic Librarianship* 42, no. 1 (2016): 55–64. *https://doi.org/10.1016/j.acalib.2015.10.008.*

Wilder Gammons, Rachel and Lindsay Taylor Inge. "Using the ACRL Framework to Develop a Student-Centered Model for Program-Level Assessment."

Communications in Information Literacy 11, no. 1 (March 2017): 168–84.

Notes

1. ACRL, *Framework for Information Literacy for Higher Education* (Chicago: American Library Association, 2016).

2. ACRL, *Information Literacy Competency Standards for Higher Education* (Chicago: American Library Association, 2010).

3. Rebecca Carlson McCall, Kristy Padron, and Carl Andrews, "Evidence-Based Instructional Strategies for Adult Learners: A Review of the Literature," *Codex: the Journal of the Louisiana Chapter of the ACRL 4*, no. 4 (2018): 29.

4. Allison Fullard, "Using the ACRL Framework for Information Literacy to Foster Teaching and Learning Partnerships," *South African Journal of Libraries and Information Sciences* 82, no. 2 (2016): 48.

5. Julia Bauder and Catherine Rod, "Crossing Thresholds: Critical Information Literacy Pedagogy and the ACRL Framework," *College and Undergraduate Libraries* 23, no. 3 (2016): 262.

6. William Badke, "DIKTUON: The Framework for Information Literacy and Theological Education: Introduction to the ACRL Framework," *Theological Librarianship* 8, no. 2 (2015): 7.

7. Kimberly Mullins, "IDEA Model from Theory to Practice: Integrating Information Literacy in Academic Courses," *The Journal of Academic Librarianship* 42, no. 1 (2016): 57. Trudi. E. Jacobson and Craig Gibson, "First Thoughts on Implementing the Framework for Information Literacy," *Communications in Information Literacy* 9, no. 2 (2015): 109.

8. Jacobson and Gibson, 105.

9. Glenda M. Insua, Catherine Lantz, and Annie Armstrong, "Navigating Roadblocks: First-Year Writing Challenges through the Lens of the ACRL Framework," *Communications in Information Literacy* 12, no. 2 (2018): 100.

10. Susan Avery, "Setting Them Up for Success: Assessing a Pre-Research Assignment for First-Year International Students," *Communications in Information Literacy* 11, no. 2 (2017): 334.

11. Rebecca Carlson McCall, Kristy Padron, and Carl Andrews, "Evidence-Based Instructional Strategies for Adult Learners: A Review of the Literature," *Codex: the Journal of the Louisiana Chapter of the ACRL* 4, no. 4 (2018): 29.

12. Yusuke Ishimura and Joan C. Bartlett, "Are Librarians Equipped to Teach International Students? A Survey of Current Practices and Recommendations for Training," *Journal of Academic Librarianship* 40, no. 3–4 (2014): 313.

Appendix 7A: Library Lab Syllabus

HTP 1105: Library Lab

Course Code: HTP 1105 (library lab) Schedule: Wednesday 4:45-5:45. Thursday 12:15-1:15. Instructor: Office Hours: by appointment. *** HTP library labs will run from the second week of classes until the 11th week.	

Description	In this mandatory library lab for the HTP foundational course the students will be introduced to the basic information literacy proficiency skills as outlined in the ACRL Framework for Information Literacy for Higher Education. We will implement several frames of the ACRL Framework by teaching students how to define their information needs, how to use mindmaps to brainstorm and visually outline their ideas, how to employ basic and advanced search strategies in a library catalogue and electronic databases, how to distinguish primary and secondary sources, the importance of academic integrity and citing sources, how to use a bibliographic management tool and the criteria for evaluating different types of sources. Students will sign up for **one** of the two timeslots available for the lab. If the dates above do not fit your schedule, contact your instructor **before the start of the course.**
Schedule	Week 1: Introduction to library resources and search strategies. Week 2: Creating mindmaps with library resources (Yewno). Week 3: Primary vs Secondary sources. Week 4: Citation Styles. (in-class quiz 1). Week 5: Using Zotero: a bibliographic management tool. Week 6: Plagiarism and Academic Integrity. Week 7: Annotated Bibliography (assignment 1 due). Week 8: Literature Review (in-class quiz 2). Week 9: Critical Evaluation of Sources. Week 10: Review + practical applications for courses (assignment 2 due).
Assessment	— Library lab is worth 30% of the final grade. — Assignments will be graded out of 100%. — 20% - Attendance/Participation. — 20% - Two in-class quizzes. — 30% - Essay on academic integrity/plagiarism (500 words). — 30% - Critical evaluation of sources assignment. — Assignments will be submitted through BrightSpace Friday at midnight on week 7 and 10.

Appendix 7B: Evaluation Rubric

HTP 1105 Evaluation Rubric for Assignment #1 Student name:
Student number:

Category	Excellent (80-100)	Very Strong: (70-79)	Developing Skills: (60-69)	Work Needed: >60
Comprehension (9 points)	Clearly demonstrates that the student has understood the concept of plagiarism and academic integrity. The student has properly addressed the research topic.	The essay shows that the student has grasped the concept of plagiarism and academic integrity. The student has addressed the research topic.	The essay shows that the student has an insufficient grasp of concept of plagiarism and academic integrity. The student has somewhat addressed the research topic.	The essay shows that the student has no understanding of the concept of plagiarism and academic integrity. The student has not properly addressed the research topic.
Research (9 points)	Student has performed a significant amount of research of the literature to answer the question (3 academic sources or more).	Student has performed adequate research of the literature to answer the question (at least 3 academic sources).	Student shows little evidence of going beyond a Google search to find internet resources (less than 3 academic sources).	Student shows little or no evidence of any research having been performed (less than 3 academic sources).
Referencing (6 points)	The essay is formatted using the APA style guide and the references are properly cited.	The essay showed a good effort at using the APA style guide and many references are properly cited.	The essay does not show an understanding of APA style and few references are properly cited.	The essay does not show any effort to apply the APA style and no references are properly cited.
Organization (3 points)	The essay structure is very clear and enables the student to answer the question effectively.	The essay structure is sufficiently clear to enable the student to answer the question effectively.	The essay structure is insufficiently clear to enable the student to answer the question effectively.	The essay structure is very unclear that it does not indicate that the student answered the question effectively.
Language and Editing (3 points)	The essay demonstrates the correct use of grammar, punctuation and spelling. The use of language is effective and clearly communicates the ideas behind the essay. No errors that interfere with the reader's understanding of the essay.	Most of the essay demonstrates the correct use of grammar, punctuation and spelling. The use of language is good and sufficient to communicate the ideas behind the essay. There are some errors that interfere with the reader's understanding of the essay.	There are several mistakes in grammar, punctuation and spelling. The use of language is insufficient to clearly communicate the ideas behind the essay. There are several errors that interfere with the reader's understanding of the essay.	There are many mistakes in grammar, punctuation and spelling. The student's use of language is insufficient to communicate the ideas behind the essay. There are many errors that interfere with the reader's understanding of the essay.

Total out of 30:

CHAPTER 8

Hands-on Learning

Using Primary Sources as Tools for Information Literacy

CHRISTOPHER ANDERSON, YALE UNIVERSITY, AND BRIAN SHETLER, DREW UNIVERSITY

*T*EACHING AND LEARNING ARE ESSENTIAL COMPONENTS TO THE MISSION of a theological school, seminary, or graduate school of religion. Planning for the implementation and use of special collections and archives in pedagogical contexts such as the classroom benefits the institution, the faculty, the students, and the library. As a result, it is essential that librarians and archivists consider appropriate venues and ways to link their resources and services to the curriculum of the school. Connecting library resources, especially primary documents and archival materials, with the curriculum can demonstrate the value of the library and showcase the educational services it provides for faculty and students. Peter Carini notes the importance of integrating primary sources into the curriculum as ways to "create expert users of primary sources" who are better prepared to "find, interpret, and create narratives using primary sources."[1] As a result, primary sources built into information literacy sessions can intersect with and be integrated into the classroom in interesting and enriching ways.

Librarians and archivists who work with special collections and archives are tasked with planning and implementing creative and engaging solutions to help faculty and students find, access, experience, and use primary resources. Special collections and archival materials intentionally integrated into the educational and curricular design of the classroom experience can help make the instructor's content more applicable to their lives. As Weiner, Morris, and Mykytiuk note, "students benefit from working with archival materials. Students who self-assess their experiences with archival research say they connected with the people whose first-hand accounts they used and that experience made history real for them."[2] At Yale Divinity Library and Drew University Library, experiences within archives and special collections function as essential components of the overall program of various departments that are charged with connecting faculty and students with primary resources. This relationship is particularly valuable as part of a curriculum and classroom experience that encompasses both institutions. Students find themselves immersed in the original documents of the past and, once exposed to these primary sources, critically engage with the materials and consider how they apply to their present situation.

Special Collections librarians and archivists who provide these services at smaller liberal arts colleges and seminaries are tasked with making faculty and students aware of the primary sources that constitute the archives of the institution, including its rare books, manuscripts, audio/visual materials, and ephemera. Bringing attention to these materials and purposefully providing opportunities for engagement with archival and special collections items and objects helps students to become familiar and comfortable with primary sources and, ultimately, informs how these same resources interact with the narrative and production of secondary sources.

Incorporating special collections and archives into coursework provides opportunities for experiential encounters with primary sources. These encounters, as Hendrickson notes, can capture students' interest and raise the level of engagement in the classroom:

> *Artifacts, material culture objects from the past, fascinate students. They are intrigued with the unknown, consumed with curiosity, and delighted to discover the true identity of these items.* [3]

Introduction and access to these materials create a sense of wonder about the past. Hubbard and Lott echo this idea, noting that "the aesthetic qualities of the items, the hands-on experience, and the act of leaving the classroom to visit a new space all seemed to generate excitement and enthusiasm in the students, which encouraged them to engage in the class investigation of the items and the discussion that followed." [4]

Using primary sources as a means of information literacy raises important historical questions for the present, helps to identify silences in historical narratives, and proposes ways of identifying and interpreting a variety of archival documents addressing social topics such as race, gender, and class. Students working with primary sources can integrate special collections and archival resources into their course projects and use digitized original materials for class presentations. Samuelson and Coker confirm: "The opportunity to examine a historical artifact and draw conclusions about its significance, assisted through carefully focused questions about the value of such objects to a modern researcher, can excite students intellectually and create a gateway through which the student may then be introduced to the concepts of the session."[5] Integrating special collections and archives into the classroom and having the materials woven into the framework of primary source information literacy can help students become better aware of the past and more critical of the present. This approach can also encourage classroom participants to critically mine and engage with materials that represent both fascinating and troubling historical narratives. These sessions can inspire and confound; they can inform while also dismantling perceptions. This chapter examines how primary sources can be used to support the framework of information literacy in theological and religious educational settings.

Primary Source Guidelines

While the *Framework for Information Literacy for Higher Education* serves as the foundational document for much of this chapter, another document is worth exploring in the context of using primary sources. Developed by a joint task force consisting of representatives from the Rare Book and Manuscript Section of ACRL and the Society of American Archivists, the 2018 *Guidelines for Primary Source Literacy* serve as a valuable complement to and supporting document for information literacy. The document was created in an effort to encourage the use of primary sources by "librarians, archivists, teaching faculty, and others working with college and university students."[6] As noted in the document, these guidelines intersect with other literacies, including information literacy. They were developed with the intention to "be flexible rather than prescriptive and were developed in the spirit of the ACRL *Framework for Information Literacy for Higher Education,* which articulates a set of interconnected core ideas, knowledge practices, and learning dispositions key to successfully navigating the information landscape more generally."[7]

With this interconnectedness in mind, the authors of this chapter have sought to approach the use of primary and archival materials through a shared lens of information literacy and primary source literacy. We see an indelible connection between the use of primary sources in both the library/archives setting and the classroom as a direct way in which to teach information literacy to students. As detailed in the *Guidelines for Primary Source Literacy,* there are a series of core concepts and learning objectives tied directly to the use of primary sources in instructional settings. The core concepts are connected to analytical skills, ethical considerations, theoretical understanding, and practical considerations.[8] These core concepts will serve as a framework for the discussion in this chapter on the use of primary sources as tools for developing information literacy. In the following section, we will explore how these core concepts can be used to support student engagement and strengthen information literacy skills. Each of these core concepts is interwoven into the six concepts that "anchor" the information literacy framework. The sections below will explore how each of the core concepts fit within these frames. Each core concept will be enhanced through the inclusion of specific examples of the use of primary sources in classes and other educational interactions.

Authority is Constructed and Contextual

At the center of this information literacy concept is the understanding by learners of what constitutes authority and how to critically question and examine that authority. This is accomplished by encouraging novice learners to "critically examine all evidence ... and to ask relevant questions about origins, context, and suitability" of the material they are encountering.[9] This process allows learners to both "respect the expertise that authority represents" and "remain skeptical of the systems that have elevated that authority."[10]

Within the realm of archives and special collections, the authority often rests with the librarians and archivists who work in the institution. For students and researchers, there is an assumption of expertise and power that is aligned with the presentation of material. It is essential, however, that new researchers who are trying to navigate this world of primary source research are aware of the parameters and limitations of this supposed authority. Those professionals who work with primary sources need to be careful not to let the age, condition, or mysterious quality of archival items serve as the reasons for their authority. Just because an item is housed in a special collections library and brought into a reading room does not automatically permeate that item with an unquestioned sense of authority. As noted in the *Framework*, it is critical that students can understand, define, and (most importantly) question the authority of an item or set of items. Not only that, but they should also question the authority of the institutions in which they encounter these primary sources. As part of this questioning, it is helpful to share with them the "behind-the-scenes" structure of the archives or special collections library such as collection development policies, donation history, and institutional purchases. It is also important to librarians and archivists to note their own role in the acquisitions process. The role of individuals in selecting material to add to collections is significant and can greatly influence the tone and tenor of the overall collecting policies. While an institution may have a particular policy or set of guidelines for collecting material, it is up to the individual curators and collection development staff to decide which items are added, kept, or discarded. In this way, the individual librarians and archivists are the initial arbiters of the institutional collections and have great influence on the material that is preserved for long-term use by students and other researchers.

At Drew University, the foregoing discussion is often connected to the Methodist Library and the United Methodist Archives. Housed at Drew since 1981, the General Commission on Archives and History (GCAH) of the United Methodist Church represents one of the largest holdings of Methodist-related archival material in the world. Drew's Methodist Library of more than 45,000 volumes serves as a natural complement to these archival materials. For students and researchers who visit the Methodist archives and interact with the material found within the building, the combined Methodist resources are unparalleled. A distinction, however, needs to be made between the archival material and the library material. It is important for the Drew and GCAH staff to explain to students what the different types of material represent and how they each have their own sense of "authority" from a research perspective. The GCAH material, for example, is mostly related to the operation of the United Methodist Church and its predecessors. Aside from a few exceptions, the GCAH does not actively collect personal papers or local church collections. This is important for students to know so they can properly understand the archive's areas of authority and collection development policies. The Methodist Library contains a wide variety of printed resources that span the full history of the Methodist movement. In many ways it is the library of record for the denomination, lending it a sense of authority and an assumption from students and researchers that the library contains "all" printed material related to Methodist history. As part of setting expectations for students, the Drew University librarians make it clear that the collection does not contain every single book ever published related to Methodism. In this way, we can help students to see that there are limitations to our own authority.

Information Creation as a Process

Students who encounter primary source material are inclined to assume that the material itself is the final product of the information creation process. A manuscript of a sermon or a letter to a family member looks, at first glance, to be a static document frozen in history. Through the extended use of primary sources, however, students begin to see that the creation process is not a single step. Rather, it is a multi-step process of "researching, creating, revising, and disseminating information."[11]

Sermon manuscripts are particularly useful in explaining the "information creation as process" core concept. By looking at these manuscripts, students can see the editing process on the page and they are required to navigate through different formats and notations to properly understand the authorial intentions of the person writing the sermon. Drew's library contains manuscript sermons of Sylvanus Griswold (1733–1819) while the Yale Divinity Library holds the sermons by Baptist minister Isaac Backus (1724-1806). Each repository contains the original texts as well as later edits and emendations. The changes reflected in these manuscripts give the documents a sense of "action" that would not be seen from a printed version of the final sermon. In addition, Griswold includes dates and places where he delivered the sermon. This information provides both context for dissemination of the text as well as giving students insight into the idea that "information may be perceived differently based on the format in which it is packaged."[12] Griswold's sermon would be understood and interpreted differently by those who heard him give the sermon versus researchers today who read the sermon (including its edits) in a library or archive.

The repackaging of information in different formats is not limited to the archival and primary source items themselves. The ways in which these items are presented to students can influence how material is viewed and understood. For example, seeing a lantern slide in a box is interesting for students to encounter, but placing the slide into a projector and seeing the image projected on a screen is a completely different experience. Similarly, the way that archivists and librarians interact with students can change how students perceive and understand primary source material. Yale Divinity Library offers live online in-class video sessions for courses at schools around the United States as part of their teaching and learning agenda. The librarian has been brought into several classrooms at Brigham Young University, Westmont College, and Albion College by means of video conferencing software. During the session the librarian walks students virtually through the Divinity Library website and presents Yale-owned digitized primary sources related to the topic of the course. These sessions encourage and enable faculty and students to identify and locate primary sources. They also identify and explain the similarities and differences between original analog-based archival objects and their digital surrogates. This distinction is important in helping them to understand the information creation process and how format (analog vs. digital) can alter the way in which a primary source document is researched and understood. One of the ways in which the librarian explores the difference between "traditional and emerging processes of information creation and dissemination"[13] is to show examples of some special collections and archival items that once existed in print but may have been lost or destroyed and are only available in a digital format. These include digitized surrogates of newspaper or periodical clippings in which the originals were digitized and then discarded during the processing of the collection. Digitization, as is explained to students, provides researchers with access to the information found within the materials without having to use the brittle and fragile newspapers.

Whether it is handwritten sermons from the 18th century, 19th century lantern slides, or long-lost archival items, the creation and dissemination process is important for students to understand and acknowledge as they explore and research with primary source documents. Through interaction with a variety of formats and outputs, students will better understand and be able to recognize how format can change the interpretation of a given resource.

Information Has Value

This core concept relates to the broad understanding that information possesses several dimensions of value, including as a commodity, as a means of education, as a means of influence, and as a means of negotiating and understanding the world. The focus of this concept is largely around attribution and citation, providing researchers with an understanding of their "rights and responsibilities when participating in a community of scholarship."[14] Researchers and students should see themselves as contributors to information and the academic environment, rather than just as consumers or users of information. Even situations in which learners are engaging with material without the express purpose of academic publication, they are taught to properly cite and acknowledge the material at hand. In archives and special collections libraries, part of the citation process is spelled out through official documentation such as finding aids. At both Yale University and Drew University, all finding aids contain citation information that students are required to use when quoting from or discussing a particular archival item. These citations are different from standard bibliographic citations such as MLA or Chicago, so staff at both institutions work with students to ensure that they understand how material is to be properly cited. This approach aligns directly with the *Framework* and its desire to encourage learners to "give credit to the original ideas of others through proper attribution and citation."[15]

The second significant aspect of this core concept is related to the idea that students need to "understand how and why some individuals may be underrepresented or systematically marginalized within the systems that produce and disseminate information."[16] Within archives and special collections libraries, this marginalization can occur both malignantly and benignly. As discussed above, collection development policies can greatly shape the overall tone and tenor of an institution. As librarians and archivists, we need to be aware of these limitations within our own institutions and explain those to students so they can understand issues related to underrepresentation. At Drew University, for example, there are tremendous holdings related to the history of the Methodist movement, but only a small percentage of those are related to African Methodist Episcopal Church (A.M.E.) history. A major part of Methodist history, the A.M.E. Church needs better primary source representation in the archives. Similarly, at Yale Divinity there is a lack of archival resources from populations who interacted with the missionaries whose collections make up a bulk of the material. Yale does not have a full sense of underrepresented indigenous individuals or groups because they are missing many of the documents of those who were the recipients of missionary work. It is important for librarians and archivists to demonstrate to and inform students how the lack of information requires the researchers to contribute to scholarship that can help fill these voids and enlarge the conversation.

Research as Inquiry

As is evident in the *Framework,* curiosity and answer-seeking is an important aspect of developing information literacy: "Research is iterative and depends upon asking increasingly complex or new questions whose answers in turn develop additional questions or lines of inquiry in any field."[17] The emphasis on open-ended exploration and engagement found within the framework aligns directly with the methodology used for primary source interaction. In particular, the focus on research is key to students' understanding of how to interact with and dissect primary sources. This is particularly evident in the use of archival material, as discussed in the following example.

Unlike most printed texts, which contain a plethora of identifying information such as author, publisher, date, etc., manuscripts are far more inconsistent in both the inclusion and placement of identifying details. A letter from a Civil War solider, for example, may include the date the letter was written but not necessarily the location of where it was written. In their role as researchers, it is important for students to know that even the most basic information may not be readily available in primary source documents such as manuscripts. At Drew University, we demonstrate this fact with a bit of a test for students. When introductory classes, such as research methods courses, visit the archives, we show them a short, hand-written note (Image 1). The note is not signed or dated and does not contain either a "To" or "From" field. Lacking this important information, the students are left to read through the note and use context clues to help them determine who the author might be. After seeing that the note contains a date (April 11, 1861), a place name (Philadelphia), and descriptive content related to a political appointment, the students are invited to take guesses.

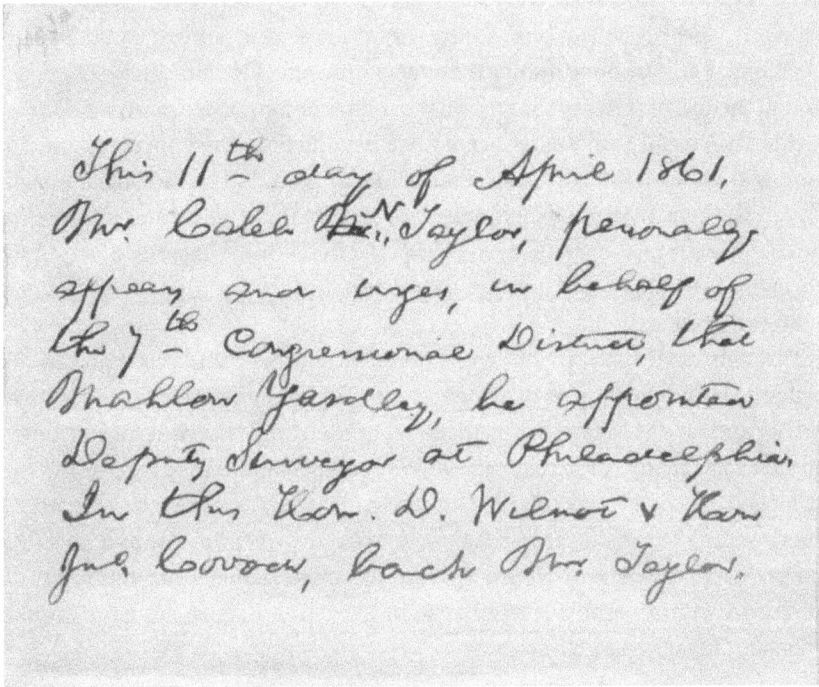

IMAGE 1 - Lincoln note, courtesy of Drew University Special Collections, Madison, NJ

Drew has used this set-up as a demonstration for students at both the undergraduate and graduate levels. Regardless of their experience or research expertise, we have found that students can readily engage with the material and think both critically and creatively in a research setting. The activity is done with groups of students so that they can help one another to arrive at the correct answer. Though it may take a little bit of prodding (or some "helpful hints" from the librarians), all groups inevitably conclude correctly that the note was written by Abraham Lincoln. Upon reaching this conclusion, students exhibit pride in their own detective skills and show an increased interest in the material itself and in the research process as a whole. In this way, we can position the concept of research as inquiry as something akin to problem-solving or even an academic treasure hunt. The pay-off for students is both obvious and encouraging, helping to strip away some of the stigma of archival research and the potentially daunting nature of working with primary sources.

Scholarship as Conversation

Visiting a special collections library or archive can provide students and researchers with an opportunity to enter a conversation with historical figures through the use of primary sources. In most interactions, these conversations can provide insights for students that take them beyond the classroom setting and the traditional understanding of information literacy. Rather than looking at material through the lens of a publisher, editor, or other arbiter of textual information, students are given a chance to connect directly with the historical actors that inform the secondary and tertiary sources that make up a good deal of their reading and research.

Through their interaction with primary sources, students can develop familiarity with the "sources of evidence, methods, and modes of discourse in the field"[18] and use this familiarity to better understand and interpret scholarly output. Particularly in situations where interpretation of sources is being challenged, having experience with these primary sources is essential to understanding "the changes in scholarly perspective over time"[19] and how these changes can influence or alter a specific discipline. This is not limited to the interaction with a particular archival item but can influence students' broader understanding of academic study:

> Connecting students with these materials early in their academic careers cannot only improve their information literacy skills, but can also enrich their learning experience in other courses, as they will be confident in their ability to access and evaluate these materials for future research projects.[20]

The interaction with primary sources can also enable and encourage students to feel more comfortable discussing their own findings and opinions and encourage scholarly conversations that "provide more avenues in which a wide variety of individuals may have a voice in the conversation."[21]

Student assignments, based in primary sources, can be an important way to develop these conversations. At Drew and Yale, librarians and archivists work with faculty members to develop and support assignments that allow students to use archival materials as a way to engage in-class readings. For example, a Media and Communications class at Drew visited the archives to look at material related to popular culture, underground publications, and fanzines. At the core of the class interaction was a focus on audience and readership. Students were asked to select an item and consider its potential audience and their overall make-up (age, gender, economic status, etc.). One of the items displayed during the class was *Motive* magazine, a Methodist publication from 1941–1972 aimed at a young adult and college-age audience. While supported financially by the church, the editorship of the magazine was made up of people who were closer in age and life experience to the intended audience. Having their peers in mind, the editors created a magazine that fit with the desires, needs, and expectations of a college-age audience. They addressed issues of concern for those in their late teens and early twenties, including topics that the church itself may not have been completely comfortable addressing (including sexuality, atheism, drug use, and anti-war protests). Students were asked to consider how audience influenced the *Motive* editors, how the church may have influenced the content of the magazine (either directly or indirectly), and how the physical format of the magazine may have influenced readership.

This assignment allowed students to bring archival material into discussion with the readings they did in class related to pop culture and audience consumption. By providing students with access to the physical material, the archives was able to encourage that dialogue between the student and the scholarly text. It helped place the student into the scholarly conversation without them feeling like they did not belong or were not worthy of participation. The archival documents themselves lend the students a sense of authority and scholarly privilege to interact within the larger scholarly discussion.

Searching as Strategic Exploration

If there is one area in which special collections departments and archives struggle with student engagement, it is getting them to walk in the door. In many cases, especially for undergraduate students, the archival reading room is an intimidating and daunting space. There is a stigma associated with the space that can prevent people, especially those who have little to no experience with archival material, from entering. At Drew, this includes the belief that "the archives is only for faculty or visiting researchers" or "that building is only for Methodists". At Yale Divinity Library, helping students overcome the perception that they are not permitted to interact with special collections items or request archival materials unless it is for serious research is a concern we attempt to address on a regular basis. Overcoming these misperceptions is the first step in making students comfortable with using primary source materials. Once we get them in the door, the next step is helping them to locate and work with the material.

Archives and special collections libraries are not like regular circulating libraries. The materials are sometimes harder to find and they cannot be checked out or otherwise circulate. While some material can be found in more traditional ILS catalogs, not everything is included in a single location. Archival collections that have finding aids are very different to navigate than a rare book collection. Teaching students the proper way to search for and access material is an essential step in the primary source information literacy process. One of the most direct and effective ways to aid in this educational process is to have one-on-one meetings with students. These reference interviews can benefit both parties, providing the student with a greater understanding of the types of materials in the archives and how to find them and providing the librarian/archivist with information about the student's project.

Working directly with students will teach them the skills needed to "search more broadly and deeply to determine the most appropriate information"[22] available for their projects. Walking students through the catalog, the finding aids, research guides, and other search tools (including some paper-based resources that have not yet been converted to digital format) will also empower students to feel comfortable doing searches on their own. Expanding search strategies and providing hints, tricks, and tips for better searching practices and patterns is essential to making sure that students can find the primary source material that they need to complete their projects or assignments.

While this close, one-on-one work with students is greatly beneficial, it is not always possible to get students to come in to meet individually. Sometimes it is necessary to go to where the students are rather than waiting for them to come to you. At Drew, special collections staff bring material out to student orientation events, open houses, admissions activities, and other events around campus. The materials, which are presented in a showcase format in table-top cases and protected from possible damage, serve as a teaser of sorts for the items that are housed in the archives building. Attendance at these events has attracted a lot of positive attention in the past few years and has resulted in both a noticeable increase in visitors to the reading room and a greater awareness of the archives around campus.

At Yale, an even more direct outreach program has reaped similar benefits. Staff at the Divinity Library bring students into contact with special collections materials in a non-traditional classroom environment. During the 2018–2019 academic year, they spoke with the chapel staff at Yale Divinity School in an effort to consider new ways to bring special collections materials into the chapel service. The result was a service built around the seven oversized volumes of the St. John's Bible. These lavishly illustrated volumes of the Biblical text written in a calligraphy style were set up at seven stations throughout the chapel and monitored by library special collections staff. Students read portions of scripture from the various volumes as part of the liturgical readings for the service. The staff highlighted the importance of care for archival items, including washing one's hands prior to working with the special collections materials. A large basin filled with water was placed outside the entrance of the chapel and several dozen towels were made available for attendees to dry their hands before interacting with the Bible. The library staff then gave a brief talk on the ritual of handwashing as part of working with archival materials and spoke about how experiencing the archive as a researcher can, for some, be a religious or spiritual encounter with the past. Students who read from the volumes actively engaged with special collections materials during the service and the remainder of the faculty and students who had attended the service were able to spend time viewing the various volumes, turning the pages and engaging with the primary sources. This not only brought material directly to the students in a comfortable and known space but also raised awareness of the types of material available for research and use at Yale Divinity Library.

From in-person visits to reference interviews to materials on display outside the library, the goal is to make items as accessible as possible and easily searchable by students. Without a clear path to locating these valuable materials, there is no opportunity for the growth in learning that primary source materials can offer. Demystifying the archives and enabling students to learn and to expand upon their strategic searching skills will allow for each of the core concepts related to information literacy that were discussed above to come to fruition. While most of the previous examples have involved library and archives staff bringing materials to the students, it is the next step in the process (enabling students to find their own material) that elevates primary source research to a level that expands and reinforces information literacy skills.

As has been examined throughout this chapter, primary sources can successfully be used as tools for the development and practice of information literacy. Specifically, special collections and archival materials can be used to support classroom learning and information literacy as outlined in both the *Framework for Information Literacy for Higher Education* and the *Guidelines for Primary Source Literacy.* The authors hope that the practical and applicable techniques presented in this chapter can aid and inspire librarians and archivists working with students in an academic and theological setting. The chapter documented several successful methods of engaging and interacting with students through the use of special collections materials and archival documents in a hands-on learning and information literacy skill-building environment. As stated in the *Guidelines,* these materials can be used as a theoretical base upon which to discuss real-world examples of how special collections and archival materials can support information literacy and ultimately help students "gain important skills that help them navigate the use of other information sources, and further develop their critical thinking skills."[23]

Bibliography

Association of College and Research Libraries. *Framework for Information Literacy for Higher Education.* Chicago: American Library Association, 2016.

Carini, Peter. "Information Literacy for Archives and Special Collections: Defining Outcomes." *Portal: Libraries and the Academy* 16, no. 1 (2016): 191–206.

Hendrickson, Lois. "Teaching with Artifacts and Special Collections." *Bulletin of the History of Medicine* 90, no. 1 (Spring 2016): 136–40. *https://doi.org/10.1353/bhm.2016.0009.*

Hubbard, Melissa A. and Megan Lotts. "Special Collections, Primary Resources, and Information Literacy Pedagogy." *Communications in Information Literacy* 7, no. 1 (2013): 24–38.

SAA-ACRL/RBMS Joint Task Force on the Development of Guidelines for Primary Source Literacy (JTF-PSL). *Guidelines for Primary Source Literacy.* Chicago: Society of American Archivists, 2018.

Samuelson, Todd and Cait Coker. "Mind the Gap: Integrating Special Collections Teaching." *Portal: Libraries and the Academy* 14, no. 1 (January 2014): 51–66. *https://doi.org/10.1353/pla.2013.0041.*

Weiner, Sharon A., Sammie Morris, and Lawrence J. Mykytiuk. "Archival Literacy Competencies for Undergraduate History Majors." *The American Archivist* 78, no. 1 (Spring/Summer 2015): 154–80.

Notes

1. Peter Carini, "Information Literacy for Archives and Special Collections: Defining Outcomes," *Portal: Libraries and the Academy* 16, no. 1 (2016): 196.
2. Sharon A. Weiner, Sammie Morris, and Lawrence J. Mykytiuk, "Archival Literacy Competencies for Undergraduate History Majors," *The American Archivist* 78, no. 1 (Spring/Summer 2015): 156.
3. Lois Hendrickson, "Teaching with Artifacts and Special Collections," *Bulletin of the History of Medicine* 90, no. 1 (Spring 2016): 136.

4. Melissa A. Hubbard and Megan Lotts, "Special Collections, Primary Resources, and Information Literacy Pedagogy," *Communications in Information Literacy* 7, no. 1 (2013): 34.

5. Todd Samuelson and Cait Coker, "Mind the Gap: Integrating Special Collections Teaching," *Portal: Libraries and the Academy* 14, no. 1 (January 2014): 62.

6. SAA-ACRL/RBMS Joint Task Force on the Development of Guidelines for Primary Source Literacy (JTF-PSL), *Guidelines for Primary Source Literacy* (Chicago: Society of American Archivists, 2018), 1.

7. SAA-ACRL/RBMS Joint Task Force on the Development of Guidelines for Primary Source Literacy (JTF-PSL), *Guidelines*, 2.

8. See SAA-ACRL/RBMS Joint Task Force on the Development of Guidelines for Primary Source Literacy (JTF-PSL), *Guidelines*, 3–4.

9. ACRL, *Framework for Information Literacy for Higher Education* (Chicago: American Library Association, 2016), 4.

10. ACRL, *Framework*, 4.

11. ACRL, *Framework*, 5.

12. ACRL, *Framework*, 5.

13. ACRL, *Framework*, 5.

14. ACRL, *Framework*, 6.

15. ACRL, *Framework*, 6.

16. ACRL, *Framework*, 6.

17. ACRL, *Framework*, 7.

18. ACRL, *Framework*, 8.

19. ACRL, *Framework*, 8.

20. Hubbard and Lotts, 35.

21. ACRL, *Framework*, 8.

22. ACRL, *Framework*, 9.

23. ACRL, *Framework*, 1.

CHAPTER 9

Reframing Information Literacy as Theological Habits

Embedding the Framework into Theological Curriculum

BRANDON BOARD, ANABAPTIST MENNONITE BIBLICAL SEMINARY

*I*N 2018, LIBRARIANS AND TEACHING FACULTY AT ANABAPTIST MENNONITE Biblical Seminary (AMBS) revised the institution's *Information Literacy Policy* document. With some additional influence from the Association of Theological Schools' (ATS) standards and its own educational goals, the seminary drew on the Assocation of College and Research Libraries' (ACRL) *Framework for Information Literacy for Higher Education* and its new definition of information literacy as a "set of integrated abilities" to embed information literacy concepts more deeply into its process of theological education.

In contrast to the idea that information literacy is solely the responsibility of librarians, AMBS teaching faculty collaborate with librarians to build and assess information literacy throughout the curriculum. Demonstration of information literacy is required for admission to the Master of Divinity program and advancement to candidacy in Master of Arts programs.

This paper will describe the conceptual background for this contextual adaptation of the information literacy framework, the collaborative process for revising the seminary's information literacy policy, and the seminary's experience implementing the revised policy in instruction and assessment activities. The purpose is to serve as a sort of case study and demonstration of the fact that ACRL's framework offers an opportunity to develop customized versions of information literacy that match the academic environment.

Background

Located in Elkhart, Indiana, Anabaptist Mennonite Biblical Seminary is a small seminary affiliated with the Mennonite Church USA and Mennonite Church Canada denominations. Originally conceived as an association between two geographically proximate seminaries, AMBS is an organization that has weathered significant change over the last few decades.[1]

One of the primary shifts to which the organization has had to adapt is a significant change in the demographics of its students. In the 2018–19 academic year, 43% of the seminary's students were not affiliated with Mennonite Church USA or Mennonite Church Canada, while about one third of the student body are from countries other than the United States.[2] An increased focus on online education and a broader recruiting net has also meant that the seminary sees fewer "traditional" graduate students[3] and more students who have been out of academia for a significant amount of time.

All of these demographic changes have underscored the importance of information literacy education and assessment for AMBS students. The first attempt at formally including information literacy came in 2006, when it was added to each degree program's educational outcomes.[4] In a 2014 presentation at the Atla Annual conference, the then-AMBS Director of Library Services Eileen Saner (who retired in 2016) discussed what each of these new information literacy program goals entailed:

> In the MA in Peace Studies and Theological Studies programs, the goal is "Demonstrate the ability to locate, evaluate, and use information effectively." The goal for the MA in Christian Formation expands the phrase, "use information and resources effectively."[5]

Within the seminary's Master of Divinity program, information literacy found its place under behaviors one would expect of practicing ministers: "demonstrat[ing] personal authority and integrity in ministry" by "knowing when to seek information and where to find it."[6]

The work to formally include information literacy as part of the seminary's curriculum alerted teaching faculty to its necessity, with some going on to describe "sloppy citation practices and greater use of inappropriate Internet resources," as well as concern over "students relying on mediocre but conveniently available Internet resources while overlooking key library holdings."[7]

The system that was put in place to address these deficiencies involved requiring students to demonstrate information literacy prior to graduation. For this purpose, students would submit a research paper for evaluation prior to graduation. A rubric was used to evaluate these papers in five key areas of information literacy:

- Ability to determine the nature and extent of the information needed
- Ability to locate appropriate information, including its authority, accuracy, and quality
- Number of sources
- Variety of sources
- Formatting of citations in footnotes and bibliography [8]

The evaluation was completed by the campus Writing Services Coordinator, who was also a student. The Writing Services Coordinator would evaluate each paper based on the five areas of the rubric, scoring each area on a scale of 0 (unacceptable) to 4 (excellent). A paper receiving a score of 2 (good) in all five categories was deemed to have adequately demonstrated information literacy, and the requirement would be satisfied. [9]

There were two significant issues with this approach. First, it kept information literacy solely in the remit of the library–and out of the hands and minds of the teaching faculty. While many professors found themselves working towards information literacy with their students regardless of the program requirements, the structure of this particular policy allowed them to not focus on it quite so carefully.

This gave rise to the second issue. With professors not necessarily working information literacy into their syllabi and not grading student submissions with an eye on information literacy, it allowed students to work their way through their programs without necessarily gaining these skills. Then, having completed all course requirements for graduation, the student would find himself/herself unable to pass the library's information literacy requirement.

As an example, consider the story of J.,[10] as recounted by current AMBS Director of Library Services Karl Stutzman:

> *J. was finishing his Master of Divinity degree at AMBS. J. completed his AMBS coursework over a number of years through work at an extension site, on-campus intensives, and online courses. J. was a first-generation immigrant from another country, where he had completed his undergraduate degree. Due to cultural differences in educational systems, J. had very little experience writing in his undergraduate degree, and those papers were written in a very different style. J.'s cultural style also made him reluctant to reach out for academic support. As part of his graduation requirements, he learned that he needed to submit a paper that would be assessed for information literacy skills, something that he needed to*

demonstrate in order to graduate. Because J.'s career as a student had spanned many years, his requirements reflected the seminary's former information literacy policy that assessed all students just before graduation. When the AMBS librarian evaluated J.'s paper, he discovered that J. could not immediately pass the information literacy assessment. The librarian worked with J. over the course of several videoconference appointments to consult about additional research materials and revise the paper to make it acceptable from an information literacy standpoint. Unfortunately, J. was almost finished with his seminary degree and was not planning to write any more papers. J. stated that he had found his writing assignments to be extremely difficult and stressful. "This would have been so helpful years ago," he remarked to the librarian. "I have been struggling all along." Although J. was able to pass the information literacy assessment and graduate, he did not gain the skills at the time in his academic career when they would have been most helpful. [11]

A New Policy

Because of J. and many students like him, it was clear something needed to be done. The policy put in place in 2006 was a start, but it was not enough. In 2016, the then-new library director Karl Stutzman began the process to reassess and revise the policy, which culminated in a full revision of the policy in the 2017-2018 academic year.

This was done with two significant goals in mind. First, the new policy needed to increase the teaching faculty's ownership towards information literacy, rather than having it function as a sort of "tacked on" program goal that was mostly the purview of the librarians. While the Association of Theological Schools considers information literacy an explicit responsibility of the library,[12] it seems that this is best done with a more holistic approach. It is "a more comprehensive project, requiring the close collaboration of a school's entire educational cohort, including librarians, teaching faculty, and academic administrators."[13]

Second, while the existing policy allowed for assessment of students' information literacy, it did not do so early enough to remedy deficiencies. As demonstrated by J.'s example, the existing policy often served merely as an additional hurdle to graduation–another box to check after all the coursework had been completed. The new policy and procedure would need to allow librarians and teaching faculty to assess students' abilities earlier in their time at

AMBS, and thereby identify information literacy issues with sufficient time to address them.

The 2017–2018 policy revision coincided with the seminary preparing for reaccreditation through the Association of Theological Schools, with the ATS self-study due in 2018, to be followed by a site visit in 2019. As the librarians and Academic Dean began reviewing the existing policy, which was part of the seminary's Academic Policy and Procedures manual, several issues stood out as needing correction. First, that manual's information literacy policy was based on the ACRL's *Information Literacy Competency Standards for Higher Education*,[14] which at that point was fairly outdated, having been replaced by their *Framework for Information Literacy for Higher Education* [15] in 2015. Librarians and teaching faculty had been utilizing *Framework* principles in the seminary's teaching strategies, but the formal policy and assessment tools remained outdated.

At the same time, the seminary's administration was working with the teaching faculty to assess the seminary's programs and curriculum mapping. This raised awareness among these key groups of the way that information literacy had previously been included as program goals for the Master of Arts and Master of Divinity programs. In an email to the author, Karl Stutzman describes some of the problems raised in this review:

> *Unfortunately, the information literacy goals were not well-represented in the curriculum map and looked like something tacked on by the library rather than something fully owned as part of the curriculum. Furthermore, it seemed we were treating information literacy as an end unto itself, as an outcome of our program rather than as a foundational skill for completing graduate theological work.*[16]

Given these realities, the seminary had arrived at an opportune moment in which to revise its Information Literacy Policy. Teaching faculty devoted significant time to this process, which included inviting the library director to discuss librarians' evolving professional understandings of information literacy. After a few rounds of proposed policy changes and additional discussion with teaching faculty, the new policy was formally approved in December 2017 and took effect beginning in the 2018–19 academic year.

The new Information Literacy Policy (Appendix 9A) is short and details three information literacy habits that AMBS students and faculty should practice:

– Critical assessment of resources' relative value and authority
– Reflective discovery of resources
– Ethical use of information

The document continues by prescribing the building and assessment of information literacy into the seminary curriculum. Before describing the educational goals which align with development of information literacy habits, the policy document provides a single sentence that radically changed the way information literacy instruction and assessment is carried out for the seminary's students:

> *Demonstration of information literacy is required for admission to the Master of Divinity program and advancement to candidacy in Master of Arts programs.*[17]

Whereas the old system required assessment at the time of graduation, this policy requires assessment much earlier in the process, typically after a given student's first year of studies. For example, in the case of a student pursuing a Master of Divinity degree, he or she must "petition for formal admission into the MDiv program after they have successfully completed 11 credit hours of study and are in process with other courses."[18] The process for students pursuing a Master of Arts degree is similar. Students pursuing MA degrees are admitted to the programs upon admission to the seminary. After completing the 11 credit hours, with additional hours in progress, "students are assessed for their readiness to be advanced to candidacy for the" Master of Arts degree.[19]

The AMBS Academic Catalog lists several criteria for faculty to consider when evaluating students' petitions for admission, or advancement to candidacy:

- Supporting evidence of the student's call to ministry
- Completion of personality inventories
- Submission of a plan for growth in spiritual formation
- Academic performance
- Recommendations from the student's academic advisor, MDiv program director, and other faculty leaders [20]

In addition to these criteria, AMBS librarians now complete a formal information literacy assessment as part of the students' admission to the Master of Divinity program or advancement to candidacy in the Master of Arts programs.

Information Literacy as Theological Habits

Arguably, one of the strengths of ACRL's *Framework* is that its "threshold concepts are not standards to be slavishly followed, but understandings that, once grasped, are reflected in the ways in which students do research."[21] This idea inspired the description of "theological habits" in the seminary's new

Information Literacy Policy. Accompanying the new policy is an *Information Literacy Scaffolding* document (Appendix 9B) which details the contexts where students can develop and utilize each habit, how these habits relate to the ACRL *Framework,* and who is responsible for developing these habits in the students.

The first habit listed in the new Information Literacy Policy is the "critical assessment of resources' relative value and authority," which is tied to the *Framework*'s "Information has Value" and "Authority is Constructed and Contextual" frames. When writing, the students should be utilizing sources with strong reputations among scholars in their fields. However, they must critically engage with these sources–not merely summarize or agree with everything. Teaching faculty work with students to develop this habit by working to learn about and evaluate appropriate sources for various types of theological scholarship, as well as by emphasizing the importance of giving proper credit for information used.

Much leeway is given to teaching faculty to determine the best way to develop this habit within their students. Because of changes in the structure of the seminary's library instruction opportunities, it has increasingly fallen to professors, instead of librarians, to discuss the different types of sources available, how to access them, and how to evaluate them. Previously, librarians conducted the typical sort of "one-shot" instruction sessions with newly-enrolled students, during which students would learn about the different types of resources available in the library and how to access them. The determination was made, however, that this fits more appropriately within the scope of work for teaching faculty, as it is a skill which must be honed. A single session during the first week of a student's seminary career, while better than nothing, is not sufficient. For example, several professors are in the habit of using class time to bring students to the library for tours of the collection. Professors use this time to show students how they (the professors) conduct their own research, which often results in explanations of various library resources related to the students' coursework. Sometimes these tours are conducted jointly with a librarian.

The second habit is the "reflective discovery of resources." Students demonstrate this habit by employing several of the knowledge practices within the *Framework*'s "Research as Inquiry" frame:

- Formulate questions for research based on information gaps or on reexamination of existing, possibly conflicting information
- Determine an appropriate scope of investigation
- Use various research methods, based on need, circumstance, and type of inquiry
- Organize information in meaningful ways

- Synthesize ideas gathered from multiple sources

Librarians work with students to develop this habit during their *Leadership in an Anabaptist Perspective* (LEAP) coursework. [22] During instruction sessions and workshops, librarians teach students about the various discovery tools available to them. This is done through exercises in which students are given sets of questions and some basic guidance about where they might find answers. Librarians work with students to nudge them in more informative directions as the students try to work their way through the library's information resources.

As students encounter resources on their journey to answer these questions, librarians help them follow the string of scholarship backwards, demonstrating the process of information creation through the scholarly conversation. Additional time is spent working with students helping them to recognize cognitive bias–do they gravitate towards sources from their own traditions because the sources align with what the students believe, or are they open to different ways of viewing and understanding the world?

The third habit in the new information literacy policy is the "ethical use of information." Since the seminary's librarians serve in an additional capacity as the writing staff, it naturally falls to them to work with students to help them learn about ethical issues related to information use. Again, librarians lay the groundwork for this habit during the LEAP coursework. Goals for these sessions are to help students recognize the various forms of plagiarism (and thereby avoid them), as well as to teach them to cite sources properly. Much of this workshop centers around an activity where students are given various essays to read. These essays are intentionally filled with various examples of plagiarism: in one essay, it might be as simple as some missing citations. In another, there are passages which are copied directly from source material, without any indication that it is anything but the author's own work. Librarians ask students to work through these essays in groups and to make note of the places where plagiarism is present. The idea being that if students can recognize plagiarism in another's work, they should be able to avoid it in their own. As students move forward in their seminary career, librarians continue to utilize their additional roles in writing support to work with students on the ethical use of information.

Assessing Information Literacy Habits

When a student reaches the point in his or her academic studies to be considered for admission to the Master of Divinity program, or advancement to candidacy for one of the Master of Arts programs, librarians solicit the submission of a research paper from the student. Students are advised that this is a requirement for their admission or advancement and are given some guidance on what to submit.

Librarians are not asking students to write an entirely new paper. Instead, students are asked to submit a research paper that they wrote and submitted for one of their classes. They are asked to think of papers which required a decent amount of research, as this gives librarians a more accurate picture to evaluate. Librarians then advise students that this evaluation does not concern the content of the paper or writing ability of the student. Presumably, the teaching faculty member who graded the assignment already gave the student adequate feedback on the content and style. Rather, librarians are assessing the ways the students used and interacted with their sources.

When students have chosen the paper they want assessed, they email the paper to a generic email address; in this case, *writingservices@ambs.edu.* Email messages to this address automatically create a work ticket in the library's writing services work tracking interface, created using the Spiceworks online help desk platform. This system allows librarians to collaborate more efficiently and ensure assessments are completed in a timely manner.

Once the paper has been submitted and the work ticket created, a librarian will "claim" the ticket and begin the assessment. The assessment is completed using a basic rubric (Appendix 9C) which closely follows the *Information Literacy Policy* and *Information Literacy Scaffolding* documents. Each of the three information literacy habits receives its own evaluation, based on the work the student has done in the paper.

For the first habit (the critical assessment of resources' relative value and authority), librarians consider three criteria. First, do the paper's sources have solid reputations among scholars? What types of sources are these and are they considered to be reputable? If not, does the student have an appropriate and legitimate reason for utilizing them? Second, does the student critically engage with the chosen sources, or does the paper merely summarize or agree with them? Some summary and agreement is to be expected, but librarians are looking to see if the students take the next step in their engagement and use the sources to inform and formulate their own ideas. Finally, does the student discuss the relationships between various sources, comparing how they are related and contrasting how they disagree? If the student has used a disreputable source, do they discuss the source's appropriateness in spite of this?

For the second habit (the reflective discovery of resources), an additional three criteria are considered. First, does the student utilize a variety of sources in appropriate formats? Librarians have found many students tend to find one or two sources with which they agree, or which they find summarize key points of their argument well, and then lean heavily on those sources.[23] Second, is the student utilizing scholarly resources available to them through the library, or are they relying entirely on materials they already have on their bookshelf at home? While utilizing materials they own is not necessarily problematic, avoiding engagement with additional scholarly resources available through the library can represent a sort of intellectual laziness, rather than the stated goal of a habit of intentional and reflective discovery of information. Third, the sources are considered for their perspective. Specifically, do the sources come from a variety of perspectives or do they all tend to say the same thing?

For the third information literacy habit (ethical use of information), librarians consider the following criteria. First, does the paper properly credit its sources for the use of ideas? Many students, especially those from different cultural backgrounds like J., find it difficult to grasp the idea of citing ideas (and not just direct quotations). Second, are the citations formatted properly? Third, does the paper paraphrase its sources in an acceptable way? Does the student concisely and accurately describe the main idea in the source material or is the source's idea misrepresented? Finally, is the student's choice of information to use appropriate to the context of the paper?

After the librarian reads the student's submitted paper with these criteria in mind, the librarian gives the paper a score of *yes, no,* or *partial* for each criterion. A student whose paper shows adequate evidence of all criteria receives a *yes* score for each, and this information is then passed on to the registrar and the student's academic advisor for use when considering the student's petition for admission to the Master of Divinity program or advancement to candidacy in the Master of Arts programs.

When a student's paper receives a *no* or *partial* score, the evaluating librarian provides additional information about what exactly was missing and how the student can go about correcting it in the future. Again, this information is then passed on to the registrar and the student's academic advisor for use when considering the student's petition for admission to the Master of Divinity program or advancement to candidacy in the Master of Arts programs.

To be clear, a paper receiving several *no* or *partial* scores will not, on its own, be enough to deny a student advancement or admission. They could serve as an additional piece of evidence in the faculty's decision not to admit or advance a particular student, but the ultimate goal of this process is not to make it harder for students to advance in their careers. Rather, the goal is to identify shortcomings in students' information literacy habits with enough time to address them before it is time to graduate.

Upon submitting an evaluation which was determined to fall short of the librarians' expectations for the students' information literacy habits, librarians are in the habit of reaching out to the student directly to discuss the results of the evaluation. Often, this is done with the intention of offering students additional counsel as they move forward in their academic careers.

As an example of how this looks in practice, consider the story of S., as recounted by Director of Library Services Karl Stutzman:

> *S. was finishing her first year of coursework at AMBS. Because she intended to study toward the Master of Divinity degree, S. needed to apply for formal admission to the program after her first year of study. S.'s work would be reviewed by the teaching faculty, who would assess whether S. had the capabilities needed to complete the program. S. was taking courses online and through on-campus intensives. In addition to her coursework, S. had a full-time job and significant responsibilities in her local congregation. Plus, S. struggled because her first language wasn't English. S. was not able to utilize the information literacy instruction she was given in one of her intensive courses; she continued to have trouble finding library resources and applying the formal requirements of the citation style used at AMBS. Because S. came to AMBS after the implementation of the new information literacy policy, her information literacy assessment was part of her process of applying to continue studying toward the Master of Divinity. The librarian evaluated S.'s research assignment and discovered it did not meet the information literacy criteria set out in the new rubric; the librarian also identified the remediation areas S. needed to work on. After reporting these results to S. and her faculty advisor, the librarian set up a videoconference to work with S. on research skills and citation formatting. After S. found additional resources and installed Zotero software on her computer, she felt more confident completing upcoming assignments in her AMBS courses. "I'm so glad for this opportunity," she said. "I really needed help with this." After the consultation, S. also felt comfortable approaching the library staff for further research and writing assistance, ensuring that she would be more likely to succeed academically in the Master of Divinity program.*[24]

Moving Forward

While not perfect, the steps taken at Anabaptist Mennonite Biblical Seminary represent an important leap forward in the way it is teaching and assessing information literacy among its students. Moving information literacy assessment into the earlier part of a student's time at the seminary has allowed librarians and teaching faculty to identify deficiencies with enough time to address them–and this is not insignificant.

However, there are still questions to work through. First, at the moment, the information literacy assessment is tied to a research paper. On one hand, this is ideal, as it allows librarians to quickly and easily identify the resources a student is using and to evaluate how the student is interacting with those resources. However, there are other types of assignments that require students to interact with library resources and that could be considered evidence of a student's information literacy. For example, a student utilizing the library's collection of biblical commentaries as part of sermon preparation should demonstrate many of the same information literacy habits as a student writing a research paper. However, depending on the student's preaching style, that student may not end up with the entire text of the sermon in written form, ready to submit to the library for evaluation. But is this student's scholarship less valuable, or less valid, merely because of a difference in format? Just because a problem is difficult to solve does not mean it is not worth solving. More careful work must be done to consider the types of work students are doing at the seminary, in addition to research papers, and make accommodations to allow these as evidence for information literacy.

Additionally, there is desire on the parts of both librarians and teaching faculty to see the partnership fleshed out more fully. Currently, much of the information literacy assessment is in the hands of librarians, while the teaching faculty handles much of the instruction. This chapter has detailed some of the ways this works and the reasons behind the decisions to structure it this way. Moving forward, this partnership between librarians and teaching faculty needs to become more collaborative, with librarians more significantly involved in instruction and teaching faculty taking a more active role in assessment.

Conclusion

This chapter has detailed a significant change made to the *Information Literacy Policy* document at Anabaptist Mennonite Biblical Seminary. Whereas the original information literacy policy required students to demonstrate their information literacy prior to graduation, the new policy moves the assessment timetable forward significantly. The intention of this move is to allow librarians and faculty to identify gaps in students' information literacy with sufficient time to address them.

In the initial year of evaluations under the new policy, feedback has generally been positive. Students have expressed their appreciation for the librarians' feedback, which often has a different tone and focus than the feedback they receive from their professors. Professors have expressed their appreciation as well. Many times, the feedback students receive from librarians echoes things the faculty have been working on, but faculty find it helpful to have additional independent voices, whose expertise differs from that of their own, offering feedback that nonetheless aligns with their own.

Bibliography

Anabaptist Mennonite Biblical Seminary. *2018–19 Academic Catalog*. Elkhart, IN: Anabaptist Mennonite Biblical Seminary, 2018.

Association of College and Research Libraries. *Framework for Information Literacy for Higher Education*. Chicago: American Library Association, 2016.

——. *Information Literacy Competency Standards for Higher Education*. Chicago: American Library Association, 2000.

Association of Theological Schools, Commission on Accrediting. *Standards of Accreditation*. Pittsburgh: Association of Theological Schools, 2015. *https://www.ats.edu/images/accrediting/documents/standards-of-accreditation.pdf*.

Badke, William. "DIKTUON: The Framework for Information Literacy and Theological Education: Introduction to the ACRL Framework." *Theological Librarianship* 9, no. 2 (2015): 4–7.

Gragg, Douglas L. "Charting a Course for Information Literacy in Theological Education." *American Theological Library Association Summary of Proceedings* 58 (2004): 50–3.

Saner, Eileen K. *Library Orientation in a New Era: A Transition in Progress, Continuing the Conversation*. *https://slideplayer.com/slide/5294755/*.

Stutzman, Karl. "Anabaptist Mennonite Biblical Seminary (Elkhart, Indiana, USA)." *Global Anabaptist Mennonite Encyclopedia Online*. March 2019. *https://gameo.org/index.php?title=Anabaptist_Mennonite_Biblical_Seminary_(Elkhart,_Indiana,_USA)&oldid=163778*.

Notes

1. The association mentioned here gave the organization its original name: *Associated Mennonite Biblical Seminaries*. This name was officially changed to *Anabaptist Mennonite Biblical Seminary* in 2012, almost 20 years after the founding seminaries merged into a single entity. For more on the history of the organization, see Karl Stutzman, "Anabaptist Mennonite Biblical Seminary (Elkhart, Indiana, USA)," *Global Anabaptist Mennonite Encyclopedia Online* (March 2019), *https://gameo.org/index .php?title=Anabaptist_Mennonite_Biblical_Seminary_(Elkhart,_Indiana, _USA)&oldid=163778*.
2. Stutzman.
3. That is, younger students moving into Master's programs immediately after finishing undergraduate work.
4. Eileen K. Saner, "Library Orientation in a New Era: A Transition in Progress, Continuing the Conversation," 274, *https://slideplayer.com/slide /5294755/*.
5. Saner, 275.
6. Saner, 275.
7. Saner, 275.
8. Saner, 275.
9. Saner, 275-6.
10. Not his real name.
11. Karl Stutzman, email message to author, March 22, 2019.
12. ATS, *Standards of Accreditation*, 4.2.1.
13. Douglas L. Gragg, "Charting a Course for Information Literacy in Theological Education," *American Theological Library Association Summary of Proceedings* 58 (2004): 52.
14. ACRL, *Information Literacy Competency Standards for Higher Education* (Chicago: American Library Association, 2000).
15. ACRL, *Framework for Information Literacy for Higher Education* (Chicago: American Library Association, 2016).
16. Stutzman, personal communication.
17. Anabaptist Mennonite Biblical Seminary, *2018–19 Academic Catalog* (Elkhart, IN: Anabaptist Mennonite Biblical Seminary, 2018), 14. Unfortunately, revision to the information literacy policy occurred too late to be included in the 2018–19 Academic Catalog.
18. Anabaptist Mennonite Biblical Seminary, *2018–19 Academic Catalog*.
19. Anabaptist Mennonite Biblical Seminary, *2018–19 Academic Catalog*, 28.

20. Anabaptist Mennonite Biblical Seminary, *2018–19 Academic Catalog,* 14–15.

21. William Badke, "DIKTUON: The Framework for Information Literacy and Theological Education: Introduction to the ACRL Framework," *Theological Librarianship* 9, no. 2 (2015): 6.

22. Taking place every August before the beginning of the fall semester, the academic catalog officially describes LEAP as "a required hybrid course that orients students to theological studies, the formation of the learning community, opportunities for personal assessment, the nature of missional leadership, and exploration of sustaining spiritual practices." Unofficially, it serves as a sort of week-long credit-bearing orientation session for new students.

23. This is especially obvious when a paper's footnotes consist almost entirely of *ibid.*

24. Stutzman, email message to author, March 22, 2019.

Appendix 9A: Information Literacy Policy

Information Literacy Policy

Revision for Academic Policies and Procedures Manual, effective 2018-19
Theological scholarship, reflection, and research require particular habits with regard to information use. AMBS students and faculty should practice these information literacy habits: 1

- Critical assessment of resources' relative value and authority
- Reflective discovery of resources
- Ethical use of information

The AMBS Library teaches these information literacy habits to all new students, using the Framework for Information Literacy for Higher Education from the Association of College and Research Libraries' as a reference point and toolkit. Teaching faculty collaborate with librarians to build and assess information literacy throughout the curriculum. Demonstration of information literacy is required for admission to the Master of Divinity program and advancement to candidacy in Master of Arts programs.
Particular educational goals in each degree program have a special resonance for ongoing development of information literacy habits. These include:

- MDiv: Graduates demonstrate personal integrity and authority in ministry
- MATPS: Graduates analyze theological and biblical foundations of peace and justice, considering Anabaptist perspectives
- MACF: Graduates reflect critically, contextually, and constructively on the theological content and practices of their specialized ministries

(Approved by Teaching Faculty, December 2017)

1. ATS Standard 4.2.1 explicitly references information literacy as a responsibility of the library. This policy accounts for the expectations of this standard and references elements of ATS Standard 3 on the Theological Curriculum.https://www.ats.edu/accrediting/standards–and–notations
2. https://www.ats.edu/accrediting/standards–and–notations 2 http://www.ala.org/acrUsites/ala.org.acrl/files/content/issues/infolit/Framework_ILHE.pdf

Appendix 9B: Information Literacy Scaffolding

Information Literacy Scaffolding

Context	Frames	AMBS IL habit	Content	Responsibility
Research Reading & Writing	Information has value	Critical assessment of resources's relative value and authority	evaluation of appropriate sources, citations	Course instructor
Leadership in Anabaptist Perspective (LEAP) – library assignment and workshop	Research as inquiry	Reflective discovery oif resources (reinforce Critical assessment of resources' relative value and authority	Discovery tools, following threads of research process, cognitive bias, tradition source come from a source "authority"	Librarians
Leadership in an Anabaptist Perpective (LEAP) – writing workshop	Scholarship as conversation	Ethical use of information	Activity on plagiarism, paraphrasing, and citation style	Writing staff
Advacement to candidacy (MA) or Afmission to program (MDiv)	N/A	All 3 habits	Assessment of academic work	The expectation is that this happens in core courses (list specifically) by the professor in that course. If students do not follow seauence, need to negotiate assessment with professor.

Appendix 9C: Information Literacy Assessment Rubric

Information Literacy Assessment Rubric

This is to be incorporated in assessment in courses that have an information literacy component. If there are deficiencies that require remediation, library and writing services staff are available to work directly with the student.

Habit	Evidence Checklist	Demonstrates (Yes/No/Partial)	If no/partial, describe deficiency to be addressed
Critical assessment of resources's relative value and authority	— Sources have solid reputation among scholars — Critial engagement with sources - not just agreement — Comparison/contrast of sources or discussion of appropriateness		
Reflective discovery of reources	— Variety of sources in appropriate formats — Sources selected from library resources and especially scholarly resources — Sources from varied perspectives		
Ethical use of information	— All sources attributed properly — Proper citation formatting — Acceptable paraphrases — Information used in context		

Karl Stutzman, March 2018

www.ingramcontent.com/pod-product-compliance
Lightning Source LLC
Chambersburg PA
CBHW031136270326
41929CB00011B/1644